THE OBERON BOOK
OF
MODERN MONOLOGUES
FOR WOMEN

THE OBERON BOOK
OF
MODERN MONOLOGUES
FOR WOMEN

Chosen and Edited by Catherine Weate

OBERON BOOKS
LONDON

First published in 2008 by Oberon Books Ltd
521 Caledonian Road, London N7 9RH
Tel: 020 7607 3637 / Fax: 020 7607 3629
e-mail: info@oberonbooks.com
www.oberonbooks.com

ISBN: 9781-814002-826-3

Cover photograph by Anna Stephens: annastephensphotography.co.uk

Printed in Great Britain by Antony Rowe Ltd, Chippenham.

Catherine has been voice coaching for over twenty years in England, Australia, Hong Kong, Africa and India. Her work has taken her into the diverse worlds of theatre, film, radio, education, commerce, law and politics. She has been Head of Voice at Rose Bruford College, Head of Voice and Vice Principal at the Academy of Live and Recorded Arts and Head of Examinations at LAMDA. Her other publications include *The Oberon Book of Modern Monologues for Men*, *The Oberon Book of Modern Duologues* and *Classic Voice (teaching vocal style)*.

INTRODUCTION

The monologues in this book have all been taken from contemporary drama published by Oberon Books. I've had a wonderful time reading through their publications list, discovering brand new playwrights and characters that just lift off the page and into your heart. And what a diverse range of female characters there are: heroines, warriors, crusaders, victims, survivors, waifs, goddesses, lovers and seductresses. Their stories range from the historical (*The Murders at Argos* by David Foley and *Camille* adapted by Neil Bartlett from *La Dame aux camélias* by Alexandre Dumas, *fils*) to fictional accounts of real women (Frida Kahlo in *La Casa Azul* by Sophie Faucher, Aung San Suu Kyi in *The Lady of Burma* by Richard Shannon and Marlene Dietrich in *Marlene* by Pam Gems) as well as the controversial (*Talking to Terrorists* by Robin Soans, *The Bogus Woman* by Kay Adshead and *Sleeping Dogs* by Philip Osment).

Plenty of resource material for performance then, whether you're an actor, director, student or teacher. To make reference easier I've organised the monologues into age-specific groups: 'teens', 'twenties', 'thirties' and 'forties plus'. However, some of the pieces aren't defined by age and cross a few of the boundaries so do spend some time reading outside of your age related box, just in case. Debbie in *Love and Money* and Hana in *The War Next Door* could just as easily be in their thirties as in their twenties, and, K Mann in *Victory at the Dirt Palace* and the woman in *13 Objects: South of that Place Near* could all be in their twenties rather than their thirties. None of these plays stipulate their characters' ages.

Monologue length varies widely depending on the material: the concise and contained to the weighty and lengthy. I haven't cut sections out of long speeches but left them intact in the hope that someone somewhere will perform them whole. Don't be afraid of adapting them to your needs however, particularly when many auditions stipulate time frames for performance.

I'm hoping these monologues will inspire you to read further and discover more about the plays they come from. Not just to gain valuable insight into your character and the story they inhabit but for the sake of a thoroughly enjoyable (and sometimes confronting) read.

Catherine Weate

CONTENTS

PART ONE: TEENS

PART TWO: TWENTIES

PART THREE: THIRTIES

PART FOUR: FORTIES PLUS

A list of the books from which these monologues are taken can be found on pages 164–167

PART ONE:
TEENS

From

THE LAST VALENTINE
by Glyn Maxwell

The Last Valentine *was first performed in October 2000 in schools in North London and at the Almeida Theatre.*

Speaking to the audience, LUCE tries to describe why she decided to write love-letters to the new boy at school in the character of Heidi, a lonely rich girl. Later, the situation backfires when she shares the story with her other school friends and they decide to set up a meeting between Ray, the new boy, and the imaginary Heidi.

LUCE

I never said I hated him. In a way
I didn't hate him at all, like I even felt
feeling for him, I mean, with wondering sort of
who he *was* exactly, because he just came
out of the blue in the winter term, and we couldn't
place the way he looked or the way he talked,
the rare times he was asked and would have to answer.
There was nothing, I mean to *go on* with this Ray,
nothing at all to go on. So one day,
not Valentine's but before, in the weeks before,
with Christmas moving away and instead of it getting
lighter, it getting colder and darker, one day
I wrote to him, to – Ray, can't say why I did it,
I didn't say who I was, or rather I did say
but what I said was I was
Heidi, I don't know why, and I said I lived
in a mansion in a great park, that I had horses
and I'm not like that at all, I never liked horses
but Heidi did, still does, and she sat in the hall
of a high white brick mansion
with pillars on the outside
at the end of a beautiful lawn and we had a pool
I told him – not that first time, that was later –
I only said I'd seen him once, down the shops,
and I wanted to be his friend. My name was Heidi.
The Friday night I posted it in the dark,
Jaz and Mish came round and I did try
not to, I mean, I did try to hold it in,
my new identity, Heidi the lonely rich girl,
sad and forlorn she sits at an upstairs window,
writing to Ray in her green ink on her special
crinkly Christmas writing paper – but then

I was miffed with them always yacking about themselves
and thinking, 'Oh she'll just listen, oh yeah Lucy,
she'll just listen and laugh!' So I did tell them.
That in a matter of hours when we next woke up,
that Ray, he'd have a new love in his life!

From

BLACK CROWS
by Linda Brogan

This play was first performed at the Arcola Theatre, London, in March 2007.

Set in 1970s Manchester, *Black Crows* explores the story of three women and their love for the one man, Marionette, who is sixteen years of age (and portrayed by a puppet in the play). HAZEL is fifteen years old and mixed race Irish/Jamaican. Her home life is difficult and she falls in love with Marionette. In this monologue, HAZEL is in the kitchen with her mother, who is drunk and about to vomit.

HAZEL

Mum, move your legs and let me get the milk.
Mum…
Mum, move over – move out of the way of the fridge.
Let me get some plain milk:
Stera's fucking terrible on your cornflakes.

It's not my fault he doesn't give you any money.

You get fucking family allowance for me.
No; but you do for the next month.
Till June – till I'm sixteen.

I'm putting them in the bin then.

Well let us get the plain.

Mum, just give us the plain milk.

You get family allowance for me.

You get family allowance for me.
They give it you for me.

I know you fucking spend it on me.

I can't fucking eat 'em with Stera on.

Right I'm getting your purse.

I'm only taking the money for the plain milk.

No I didn't.

You did it yourself.

No I didn't.

Mum I didn't.

It won't bruise.
I didn't mean it.

Tell me dad what you like.

All he'll say is go up the stairs.
'You no hear me go up the stairs.'
And I will.

No I don't.
I'm hardly ever here.

Are you gonna give me the plain milk or not?

Fucking stick it then.

As long as you get family allowance for me I'm staying.

You're just as bad.

You're every bit as bad.

I'm not going till I've done me O Levels – I'm going to
university.
One month, one fucking month and then I'm out of here.

Mum, move away from the fridge.
Mum, lean over the sink.
Lean over the sink.
Mum, lean over the sink.
If you don't lean over the sink…
Lean over the sink.
Please.
Will you lean over the sink.
Take your glasses off.
Take your glasses off.
Take your glasses off before…
Let me take your glasses off.
Look. Look there. LOOK THERE NOW.

Sit up or you'll choke.
MUM, sit up.
Will you sit up.
Where's your knickers?
Where's your fucking knickers?

I can see all your…

SIT UP.
Fuck you then.
You stupid old cunt.
FUCK YOU THEN.
You drunken old…

It's alright – it's alright – we'll clean it up.

From

THE MURDERS AT ARGOS
by David Foley

Originally commissioned by the Hyperion Theatre in Seattle,
The Murders at Argos *was first performed at the New York
International Fringe Festival in August 2000.*

David Foley, an American playwright, has updated the Oresteia
for modern day audiences. Orestes has killed his mother and
her lover to avenge the death of his father and is now on trial.
His sister ELECTRA supports him and, in this scene, speaks to
Tyndareus, her grandfather, in front of everybody, about who is
really to blame for the tragedy.

ELECTRA

(*To* TYNDAREUS.) *Where is your shame?* Any of you? How dare you stand here and pretend to judge him? You talk of law and justice as if you knew what those words meant. Where is your shame!

If you kill my brother it won't be because of his alleged crime. It will be because he is an inconvenience to you. He is a sign of *your* disease and *your* corruption, and you'd just as soon not have to look at him.

Where was your justice when my father was murdered? Where were your noble ideals then? They weren't convenient. My mother was powerful so you laid aside your scruples and pretended nothing had happened. But now my brother comes and rights a terrible wrong, and you fall on him like birds of prey. Justice indeed!

How I admired you once. The brave men of Greece, sailing off to war. So strong. So glorious. I *believed* in you!

And now you've come back – the world laid waste because of you – and you dare to judge *us*?

You have failed us, your evil generation. You have bred us up in violence. You have made a religion of it. Then when *we* are violent, you turn on us. You tell us we're diseased and unnatural. Well, if we're diseased, who were the carriers? Who infected us?

If Orestes is guilty, then so are you. Condemn Orestes and you condemn yourselves. Remember, we are your children.

Her voice breaking a little.

We are your children.

A last childish whisper.

We are your children.

From

SMALL MIRACLE
by Neil D'Souza

Small Miracle was first performed by the Mercury Theatre Company at the Mercury Theatre, Colchester, in June 2007.

The play is set in a caravan park in Knock, County Mayo, Ireland, which has been a Catholic pilgrimage site since the miraculous appearance of the Virgin Mary over one hundred years ago. SADIE is thirteen years old and on holiday there with her Irish mother, Bronagh, her Hindu step-father, Arjun, and her Hindu grandmother, Meera. The road trip has brought out the worst in everybody and the family is at 'war' with each other. On top of this, SADIE was recently traumatised by the death of her best friend, Derbhle, and Derbhle's boyfriend Noel, in a car accident (SADIE was thrown free of the burning car). However, she continues to call Derbhle's answering service to 'talk' to her. At the same time, SADIE finds a new best friend to play with in the adjoining field. Is this mysterious new friend real?

Or is it another vision and miracle? No one is quite sure.

SADIE

I have to whisper. I'm sneaking a fag. I have so got to cut down, but God I need this. (*She takes a drag.*) Just to say Greetings. The story so far: Mam's being a bitch, Arjun's running after her like a poodle, and I made a new friend. She's great like, really fantastic. I was going to write you a postcard, but my arm fell off, so I'm leaving you this message. Laters.

She hangs up. She has a drag on her fag. Then she hits recall and puts the phone back to her ear.

(*Pause.*) Me again. Forgot to say, was it you I saw with Noel O'Sullivan on Dame Street last Friday? I was on a bus and you were standing in the rain. I shouted from the bus, but you didn't turn round. Why didn't you turn round? I was jumping up and down like trying to get yer attention. I was like yer man outside Easons on O'Connell Street, yer man with the pissy trousers, who dances like a mad thing. People must have thought I was mad, but you didn't turn round. (*Beat.*) Too interested in Noel, I bet. Noel eh?! The God of Sex! Remember how we gave him the 'Most Promising Arse In Jeans' award last year? Saying that he's not really my type. I can see why you like him though. No, his brother Kieran was always more my type. Hey would you get Noel to put a word in? Drop my name into conversation, in passing like, see what he says, or does, or the expression on his face. And don't make it obvious like you did with Peter Hickey cos I couldn't get rid of him then for a term and he'd a face like a gorilla on heat. I'm relying on you now as my friend. My best friend.

She hangs up. She has another drag on her fag. Then she hits recall again, puts the phone back to her ear.

(*Pause.*) Jesus Derbhle answerphones I hate them! I forgot to say what happened this afternoon. I had this blackout thing. It was mad: one minute I was there. The next I woke up in bed with everyone round me, and Mam holding my hand crying and a doctor there as well. Thing is she was there when it happened, my friend. She's great, amazing. She listens to everything I say and she's so beautiful. You'd love her. She's there now. Waiting for me in the field. I have to go and see her. Just thought I'd say a quick hello. (*Beat.*) Look, I know you've been busy with stuff and that's why you haven't got back to me, but when things calm down, you will call me, won't you? And we'll hang out like we did before? (*She notices something offstage. A light.*) That's her now. I have to go. I'll call you again, but you know how it is with Mam. She hates me calling you cos she knows I can talk to you. And last week she said she'd throw me out of the house if she ever caught me calling you again and I said, "Do it!" Cos when I'm gone, I'm never coming back. Never! I'll be away Derbhle, away like you. Just like you.

From

A BRIEF HISTORY OF HELEN OF TROY

by Mark Schultz

This play was originally produced in the US by Soho Repertory Theater with True Love Productions Inc. and was first performed in the UK at Drum Theatre, Plymouth in September 2005.

A Brief History of Helen of Troy or *Everything will be Different* is written by the American playwright, Mark Schultz, and explores the world of fifteen year old CHARLOTTE who is grieving over the death of her mother. She focuses on Helen of Troy for a school project and wonders if Helen's daughter, Hermione, feels the same pain and loneliness that she does. Heather is an imaginary friend who makes CHARLOTTE feel worthwhile; however, towards the end of the play, CHARLOTTE realises that she has to give her up if she is going to move forward with her life. She picks up the phone and acts out this imaginary conversation with her.

CHARLOTTE

She looks for the phone. Finds it. Holds it. Picks up the receiver. Sets it down again. Beat. She disconnects the phone. Picks the receiver up again. Puts the receiver to her ear. Does not dial. She is beginning to break. She struggles with composure throughout.

Um. Heather? Um. Hi. Um. Hi. Heather? Um. Everything's okay. It's really okay. Um. I just had to call. And. Um. How was your weekend? Good. I hope. I would love to have visiting cousins from Czechoslovakia. That would be. So fun. I think. You're so so wonderful.

I don't think. I don't know. Um. I think maybe it would be good. Maybe. If I didn't see you. Anymore. For a while. Maybe for just a little while. 'Cause I think. Maybe. For just a while. I should maybe try. Um. Try stuff without you? Please don't be mad. I don't want you to be mad. It's not like. Please don't be mad. I've. I just have to think through a few things. And I think I could do that better if maybe you weren't around. For a while. For a long time. Probably.

And I know. I know. I know what you're thinking. I'm a loser. I'm such a fucking loser. I'm an ugly fucking stupid fucking ugly fucking loser. And you're right. You are so right. And I can't do it on my own. And people will hate me. And laugh at me. And I'll be lost. I know. I'll be lost. Without you. I know it. You are my life, Heather. You are everything. I want. And I wish. I could keep you. Close to me. And this is so hard. This is so hard. Please don't yell at me. I feel like I'm dying. I love you so much.

I'm gonna try to make it to Mexico. To see you. One of these days. I figure you'll probably move there. Soon. But I'll visit. It just might take longer for me. This way. To get there. Without you. But I think it'll be better. I think. I hope it'll be better. This way. But so hard.

You made me feel so beautiful, Heather. Thank you. And goodbye. Goodbye.

She hangs up. Picks up the receiver again.

Heather?

She hangs up. Picks up the receiver. Listens.

Mama?

She sets the receiver down slowly.

(*Almost a whisper.*) Daddy?

Beat. She bursts into tears.

From

GLASS EELS
by Nell Leyshon

Glass Eels was first performed at The Brewhouse Theatre, Somerset in June 2007.

Set in the Somerset Levels, *Glass Eels* tells the story of LILY who is struggling with the first stirrings of her sexuality whilst living in an all male household. LILY is drawn to the river near her home where her mother died and where thousands of eels are also stirring, ready for their long migration to the Sargasso Sea. The only person she is able to make any connection with is a family friend, Kenneth, who has known her all her life. It is night and LILY and Kenneth are down by the river, sharing their stories of loss.

LILY

I think I'm like my mother.

She came down here at night.

I know I shouldn't come, but I can't stop myself.

I know she came here. Sat here. Swam in there.

She's not in the house anymore.

I used to look for her. I found things she touched. I found a piece of paper with her handwriting. I found a shoe in the garden. A dress she'd worn.

It hadn't been washed.

LILY sits up.

I want to tell you this thing. But I don't want you to look at me.

Look away. That's it.

If you look at me I'll stop.

I used to think everyone had dead bodies in their houses. I'd go in the room where he got them ready. He caught me one day, looking at the powder he used on their skin to tighten it. I was gonna use it on me but he took it from me, said it was only for dead skin.

I started going down at night and if we had one in I'd lift the sheet from their faces.

I used to think if I looked at them long enough I could bring them back to life, make them breathe again.

One night there was a new one there. I took the sheet and peeled it down. Stood and stared.

It was my mother.

KENNETH *looks*.

No. Don't look at me.

It had happened late at night and no-one had woken me to tell me. That's how I found out.

Her skin was streaked with mud. Her hair still damp from the river. A piece of weed in it.

Pause.

I stood there and tried to make her breathe again. Tried to make her chest move.

Nothing happened.

So I reached out and pulled her eyelids up, to get her to open her eyes and look at me. But her eyes had rolled back and there was just the whites.

I tried to pull the lids back down but they had stuck.

I had to go upstairs and into my dad's room. I had to tell him to come with me, to see what I'd done.

He followed me down and I showed him.

He saw and then he turned and grabbed my arm, too tight. He shook me and screamed at me, told me I shouldn't have gone in. And then he hit me. Here. (*Touches face*.)

Some things that happen to you, you get them in here. (*Touching head*.) And you can't get them out.

I wish you could take it out so I didn't have to remember it.

From

HANNAH AND HANNA
by John Retallack

Hannah and Hanna *was first performed at the Channel Theatre Company Studio in June 2001. It is published in* Company of Angels, *which includes three other plays by John Retallack:* Club Asylum, Virgins *and* Risk.

Hannah and Hanna focuses on the tensions that occurred between asylum seekers from Kosovo and English locals in the seaside resort of Margate. HANNA is a sixteen year old Kosovan who ends up in Margate with her mother and brother, Albin. They receive verbal abuse from the locals (including a sixteen year old English girl called Hannah) who feel threatened by the large numbers of asylum seekers placed in the town. However, Hannah and HANNA do eventually bond, primarily through their love of pop music. Just as the tensions start to increase, Hannah's brother, Joe, a local policeman, takes HANNA's family back to Kosovo, with medicine for the hospitals there. Hannah hides in the back of the truck. In this scene, they stumble across a burnt out coach by the side of the road. HANNA explains to Hannah what happened when they tried to escape to Macedonia in it.

HANNA

That's the coach.

We left for Macedonia in that coach;
It was our escape from Kosovo,
The beginning of our journey to Margate.
We were stopped by the Serbs.
They were selecting young people;
Albin and I were both chosen.
My mother was still in that coach.
They would not let her off.
The men were taken off first.
The women were taken to a garage
Twenty minutes down the road,
A big empty building.
The soldiers all had knives and guns;
All were wearing masks.
My clothes were torn off me.

   She stops.

At some point the screaming around me stopped;
I think the soldiers got some sort of order.
I do not know why they set us free.
We were taken out of the garage, back to the roadside.
We smelt the coach burning before we saw it.
We met up again with the men.
Albin was there and though he was beaten
He was standing.
He was alive.
I was ashamed for him to see me like this,
But he saw I was alive too.
Not all of the men were there.
The coach was still in flames.
The Serbs made us walk to Macedonia.

I did not know if my mother was dead in the coach.
When I got to the camp in Macedonia I was very bad.
My mother was waiting for us.
She was alive.
She looked after us.
She helped me not to be ashamed.
I cried for weeks and my mother said:
'Don't stop, cry more.'
And hugged me.
When Albin told me about a lorry going to England
He said it was the first time that I smiled again.
We could go to England.

From

VIRGINS
by John Retallack

Virgins *was first performed at the Junction Theatre, Cambridge, in July 2006. It is published in* Company of Angels, *which includes three other plays by John Retallack:* Hannah and Hanna, Club Asylum *and* Risk.

Virgins is described as a 'family drama about sexual politics', which explores some of the issues surrounding teenage sexual experimentation. Fifteen year old ZOE is home from the same party that her brother Jack attended. They both met someone special there although ZOE's experience was a lot more innocent than Jack's. She speaks as she writes in her diary.

ZOE

I'm writing my diary for the week while it's calm
Mum and Dad aren't up yet
I fed the cat
Jack is asleep
And because he forgets to turn his alarm off at weekends
It went off at seven
It went off very loud
Right next to his ear
I'm the one who has to go and stop it

He's lying there fully dressed
With the sun full in his face.
His clothes and his hair stink of smoke and drink –
He's only been back a short time
I was at the same party
And I left it a whole day earlier

He's alive
Just dead till the afternoon

I like it when everyone's asleep
The quiet is different to other quiet
It's Sunday quiet.

I met a boy at the party.
He's got manners
He's incredibly polite;
He's tall and thin with deep brown eyes
He's been in England for two years
His parents are dead
He told me
That's why he's here,
His uncle and aunt live in Southside.

He came to the party but it's not his scene
When you see it through his eyes
You can see why it's not.
He doesn't drink for a start and drugs just aren't on his list.
He's got self-control,
Not like Jack and his mob.
They *stampede* the girls,
They're in such a rush
They don't know what they're doing
This boy – he's beyond all that.
He's calm; he's not hurried,
He's not thirsty all the time like the rest of them
He doesn't smoke either.
He has a sweet scent about him.
I can't work out what it is –
I want to know
I want to buy it and wear it on *me*.
Calm, calm.
It'll take time.
If he is to trust me
I will have to be patient and calm too
I want to know him better,
Much better than I do now,
I've been thinking about him all night.
I don't know his name.
He kissed me goodbye.

   Gestures.

Just here.
That was so *nice*.

From

RISK
by John Retallack

Risk *was first performed at the Tron Theatre, Glasgow, in February 2007. It is published in* Company of Angels, *which includes three other plays by John Retallack:* Hannah and Hanna, Club Asylum *and* Virgins.

Risk grew out of interviews with teenagers in Glasgow and explores why young people want to push boundaries and what they risk losing in the process. ANNMARIE is high on life and enjoys going out without having to get drunk and stoned, unlike her friends. She soon finds herself under pressure to conform.

Her story is told directly to the audience.

ANNMARIE

It was the first time I went out in a group with my friends.
It was a really big club, 'The Garage'.
Everyone was taking something,
All my friends were out off their faces
I was sober and I didn't snog anyone.
I just danced all night.
Every time we all went out together,
It seemed to go like that.
They all got wiped out and I didn't.
I never drank or took anything.
Some of my friends started on at me –
Why was I cool and in control, always?
While they were getting wrecked?
Was I mean? Or scared?
Why was I always such a good girl?
I said to them I like clubbing,
I'm having a great time –
Leave me alone.
And it was always me who was there
To scrape the puke from out their hair,
To protect them from blokes,
To tell them where they lived
And I got them home too, by cab;
They wouldn't remember that the next day
Or believe that it had cost a tenner.
They thought I just wanted to be in control of them;
I was too scared to 'let go'.
I said I let go completely when I'm dancing.
They said I never joined in.
That was rubbish and I told them so
And I just kept on dancing.
But they didn't leave off.

They started to wind me up.
They said I was a goody two-shoes.
They called me a stuck-up.
Well that was too much.
I am not stuck-up.
So one night I had a pint and a smoke –
In front of them all.
They all gasped and cheered.
I went to the toilet and threw up.
When I came back they were all watching to see what I'd do.
I bought a round and had another pint.
My rating went right up.
They hugged me, congratulated me.
After that whenever I went out with them,
If they got pissed, I got pissed with them.
And I couldn't remember how *I* got home,
Or what I'd said or what I'd done or who I'd done it with.
Thing was, it seemed a bigger risk to be sober than be drunk.

And once I'd started drinking, I stopped dancing.

From

ROSALIND
by Deborah Gearing

Rosalind: A Question of Life *was first presented by Birmingham Repertory Theatre on a schools tour in September 2005. The first public performance by Birmingham Repertory Theatre was at The Door in November 2005.*

Rosalind: A Question of Life tells the story of Rosalind Franklin who helped discover the structure of DNA only to be written out of the history books. ESTHER is in her late teens and is studying to be a scientist. She is convinced that biochemistry is the way forward but her brother, Joe, isn't sure and raises some moral dilemmas. Then Rosalind appears and they find themselves re-enacting her life and entering into the debate. In this scene, Joe and ESTHER are remembering the time ESTHER lost a science quiz when she was fourteen.

ESTHER

I flunked it, Joe. But not because of that boy. I lost my concentration. I was too tired or something. Somebody coughed. And it was you, Joe.

You coughing. And then I looked. And you looked just like dad – and I felt this terrible – whoosh – I missed dad. It went right through me.

It's funny how things flash through your mind sometimes – how quickly you can think – like three films at once, all playing at once. I thought so many things in thirty seconds – I remembered when I said I wanted to be a scientist at tea one day. And they laughed and said – you could be a doctor. That'd be good, a doctor in the family. And I said – no – I want to be a research scientist – work in a lab, do experiments. And dad said – it will be useful, won't it? Is that useful? And you sat there in the audience, coughing just like dad, and I couldn't believe he'd gone. It was like he was in the room. And then I remembered coming home from school, and gran was sitting there crying. And I'd never seen her cry before. And it was all creepy quiet. No radio. She always had the radio on. Crying for her boy. My dad. He'd had a massive asthma attack and his heart had given way. His poor heart. And then you came home and she had to tell it all over again. And it didn't change, the way she told it – it was like – she couldn't find any other words to say it. There just aren't any other words.

My boy, she said. My boy.

And so – when I heard you coughing I just suddenly missed dad. And it was quiet around me, I was far away. And I didn't care about winning. I just really didn't care. I just wanted dad back.

From

BREATHING CORPSES
by Laura Wade

The first performance of Breathing Corpses *took place at the Royal Court Jerwood Theatre Upstairs in London in February 2005.*

Breathing Corpses takes its title from Sophocles' assertion: 'When a man has lost all happiness, he is not alive. Call him a breathing corpse.' The play follows a gruesome cycle of linked deaths and how they affect the living. AMY is a nineteen year old chambermaid in a mid-price hotel. She lets herself into one of the rooms to clean only to discover a dead body in the bed. This is the second time it has happened to her and she wonders whether she'll lose her job over it. So she talks to the body whilst trying to pull herself together.

AMY

I'm OK.

Amy wipes her eyes and smiles weakly.

Just – you're dead and I'm going to get sacked I think, so
– Not very – not very good, is it?

She laughs at herself.

Talking to you.

She frowns, looking around the room.

That's new.

She sighs and turns back to the corpse.

What's your name, Mr Man?

She turns back to the bed, pretending that the corpse spoke.

I'll go down and tell them in a minute. Probably think I'm
joking this time.

Beat.

Amy sees an envelope propped up on the dressing table.

Oh, you did a letter. Nice.

Amy picks the envelope up.

You know you look – I bet you were lovely. I bet you were
really – really kind.

Not a person I'd ever really talk to but. But you look lovely.
Don't fancy you or anything, you're a bit old for me. Probably
got kids my age. Oh god have you got –

Beat. She looks at the envelope.

Does it say in here? Who's Elaine?

She turns the envelope over in her hand.

You didn't lick it. You know they'll take this. Evidence. She'll not get it for days. She'll have a few days of not knowing why, while they're doing tests on it and stuff. If you've said why in here.

D'you mind if I – It's just you've not sealed it, so no-one'd know, cept you and me and I won't tell anyone if you don't.

Amy opens the letter and turns it over to see the name at the bottom.

Jim. Hi Jim.

She reads the letter.

Oh my god. A woman in a *box*. Like a cardboard box? God. Yeah, that's really hard. Hard enough finding you, can't imagine if I found one in a box.

Didn't you wonder about who was going to find you?

Amy finishes the letter.

That's a really nice letter, Jim. I mean, you know… For that kind of letter it's nice. Not too long, you don't blame anyone. Wouldn't seem fair, really, they never get chance to say anything back. Good you haven't blamed anyone.

D'you mind if I open the window? It's just you smell a bit. No offence, but. It's just – You've had a stressful time, what with the – (*Gestures to the letter.*) and I think you've – on the sheets, so –

She opens the window.

Cold out there.

Don't want to smell nasty when they come in, do you?

From

STAMPING, SHOUTING AND SINGING HOME
by Lisa Evans

Stamping, Shouting and Singing Home *was commissioned and first performed by Watford Palace Theatre-in-Education Company in 1986.*

The play is set in 1950s America and Lizzie and her family are still experiencing the everyday injustices reserved for black Americans in the Deep South. However, the world is on the brink of change and Lizzie's older sister MARGUERITE decides to fight back. In this speech, she describes for her mother and Lizzie what happens when she tries to eat in a café usually reserved for white people.

MARGUERITE

I didn't plan on staying out late Mama. It was light when
I went in. It was real crowded but only a few folks sitting
outside at them pretty tables on the sidewalk. So I went and
sat there too. Folks were staring like I come from Mars or
someplace. You think my skin green not brown. But I didn't
take notice. I sat at the table and waited for the waitress.
Pretty soon she come out and took an order from the table
next to mine. Then she goes back inside. Through the glass
I could see white folks nudging and laughing at me, and the
waitress talking to the manager. She come out with the order
for the next table. This time I say, 'Excuse me Miss.' But
she act like I wasn't there. No voice. No sound. But I heard
my voice. And I heard it again when next she pass and I say,
very polite, 'I'd like a cup of coffee, please.' I ask three more
times but she carries on acting like I'm invisible. Then it come
on to rain. But I sat on. I sat on while it got dark and they
turned up the lights inside. And folks came and went and had
coffee and cake and talked and laughed together. And I sat on.
Pretending I didn't care. They weren't going to drive me away.
Flood could have come and I'd have stayed, sitting in the dark,
rain on the window panes, running down my back till I didn't
rightly know if I was turned to stone. Some cars hooted as
they drove off, laughing and yelling foul words. But I sat on. I
had a right to be sitting there. I had a right to be served coffee
just like they did. So I sat on. Then they closed up, put out
the lights. I got up and come home.

PART TWO: TWENTIES

From

CRESSIDA AMONG THE GREEKS
by David Foley

Cressida Among the Greeks *was first performed at the Ohio Theatre in New York City in February 2002.*

Cressida Among the Greeks is an updated version of Shakespeare's *Troilus and Cressida* and explores love and betrayal amidst the chaos of war. The god Apollo gave the gift of prophecy to CASSANDRA, Troilus' sister, but also made sure that her visions of the future would not be believed. CASSANDRA foretells the downfall of her family and the city of Troy, which is currently under siege from the Greeks but, of course, no one will listen to her.

CASSANDRA

I guess my mistake was not giving in. You can't play footsies with a god. They don't like being toyed with, gods.

Oh, I thought I was so smart! Here's this god – Apollo, if you please – wants to give me the Gift of Prophecy. And all he wants in return is I let him do me. Big deal. But no! I'm too smart for that. I tell him sure, no problem. Then when he's come just close enough to fill my mouth with the future – when I've lapped it off his tongue – then I snap my legs shut and say, Nothing doing! Gotcha, sucker!

Clever girl.

Too clever.

What was I thinking anyway? The gift of prophecy? Why? Who needs it? To know more than the dumb blind lot of humans – is no gift. Knowledge is power – yes. But, there, you know – that's where he got me. Knowledge *without* power. To know, to tell, but never to be believed – there's nothing so powerless as that. The vision all interior – terrifying, shattering – and all *inside*. It *is* a kind of madness. A barren, cold and windswept place where no one comes – but me. If a thing can't be told – can it be real? And if not real, of course it's…

Pause.

I should have fucked him. What was my problem? I mean, he was a god. How bad could it have been? And one quick poke would have saved me a world of trouble. What was so precious I couldn't give him what he wanted? My virginity? What's that? Who cares? You want it? Take it. It's his. It's yours. It's anybody's. I'd take anyone on. I'd fuck 'em all – if just for a moment, I could see the blood and horror fade – just for one moment – a peaceful brain…

From

NAVY PIER
by John Corwin

Navy Pier was first produced by Wax Lips Theatre Company in October 1997 at Strawdog Theater, Chicago, Illinois. The production then moved to the Live Bait Theater, Chicago, Illinois in January 1998.

Martin has just moved to San Francisco and takes on the persona of his once best friend, Kurt, with whom he went to college with in Chicago. Martin and Kurt were fellow aspiring writers but Kurt left Martin behind when he had a short story published in an important magazine and moved to New York to make a name for himself, taking Martin's girlfriend, Iris, with him. Martin thinks that Kurt's personality was the key to his success and tries to emulate him. He meets LIV in a bar, where she works as a waitress, and asks her out using Kurt's name. However, he realises that this is a mistake so he doesn't show for the date. He turns up at the bar the following night and, here, LIV explains what happens next. She speaks directly to the audience.

LIV

Martin said he was very sorry but he lied to me, about who he was, and he didn't want to lie to me or to anyone else anymore about who he was, and if I gave him just half a chance, he'd never lie to me again, about anything, and I would never regret it.

Pause.

This *guy*…

Everything in me told me to just walk away, forget the whole thing. But…there was something about him…

Pause.

So I told him I would think about it. You know. And he said he understood. And after that, he would come into the bar once a day. Hand me a manila envelope. And then he would walk out the door. Without a word.

Pause.

And inside the envelope was…a story, I guess. Or a poem. Little paragraph. Whatever. Each day it was something different.

He wasn't trying to 'woo' me. He was just trying to…let me know who he was. Or who he might be.

Pause.

And on Fridays, after I had been off work for four days, he would bring in four envelopes. It got to be so that Friday was my favorite day, four envelopes, four slips of paper – My favorite one was only four words long, centered in the page. 'I love your hips.' Imagine that. Someone loving these hips.

Pause.

So anyway. It lasted four weeks. Until I finally gave in. Agreed to go out with him again. Or for the first time.

Pause.

And, as it turned out, we had a great time. Great.

From

LOVE AND MONEY
by Dennis Kelly

Love and Money *was first performed at The Studio, Royal Exchange Theatre, Manchester, in October 2006.*

Set in contemporary London, *Love and Money* explores how money (or the lack of money) has an impact on love and relationships and, in so doing, takes a swipe at the modern workplace. DEBBIE is meeting with Duncan in a 'shitty pub'. Although the meeting is never explained in detail, we learn, when Duncan shows her a picture of two men engaged in oral sex, that DEBBIE might be looking for an alternative way of earning money. Duncan tries to learn a little more about her and wants to know something that she has never told anyone else before. Debbie responds with this monologue, which explains her feelings for her current job.

DEBBIE

I put wall-paper paste in the coffee machine at work.

Beat.

You know the powder, you buy the powder in, while no-one was looking I put it into the machine and stirred it all in and left it and it clogged up the machine and they all stood around it staring at it, hurt, like it was a dead puppy.

Beat.

When you print orders at work, they come out face up with the address on, on, on the front and you never see the backs until they, you know, come back from the clients completed, the order form is on the back, you see, so you never see the, until, so I stayed late one night and I photocopied the word 'cock' on the back of all the order forms, with a big picture of a cock and balls that I drew in magic marker, and then I put them back in the printer, and the next day they sent out thousands and they got hundreds of complaints and lost their two biggest clients.

I keep falling asleep in meetings and no-one's noticed yet. They think I'm concentrating.

Last week I caught a mouse in my flat, I have mice, which is something I don't really, I don't really like that, I have mice and I caught this one on glue paper, you know, the glue traps, I've tried everything else and that's the only thing that works and the worst thing is that when you catch them they're still alive so you have to, you know, despatch them, so I put a cloth over it and I hit it on the head with a cup, a mug, but it took quite a few, you know, hits and it was screaming and I felt sick and I was crying and everything and then I peeled it off the paper, you have to be very careful because the body's quite delicate, and then I took a scalpel that I have for handicrafts and I slit its little belly open and I tugged out all its insides and I stuck them and the body onto this Christmas card, so that it was splayed open with the guts out into this Christmas tree design, and I sent it to my boss with writing cut out from a newspaper saying 'Thanks for all the hard work and good luck in the new job cunt-face'. They called the police.

Beat.

I wanted to be a newsreader when I was a little girl.

From

LA CASA AZUL
by Sophie Faucher
(translated by Neil Bartlett)

The translation of La Casa Azul *was first performed at the Lyric Hammersmith in October 2002.*

La Casa Azul is the story of the Mexican painter, FRIDA KAHLO and is named after her blue house in Coyoacán, near Mexico City. The play explores her struggle with her husband (the painter, Diego Rivera), her body (after a horrific accident), her country and her art. In this speech, FRIDA is alone: Diego left her after an argument about his inability to be faithful. His latest conquest had been FRIDA's sister, Christina. She cuts off her hair, which he loved, to spite him.

FRIDA

This dark night of mine beats like a wounded heart. It has no moon…

This dark night stares wide-eyed at the window, stares blankly at that faint grey light. This night is long, so long and it leads me I know not where. You are gone, and this night hurls me down into that great pit. I reach for you, reach out for that great fat body next to mine, the sound of your breathing, your smell, and the night replies: the bed's empty; I've got nothing for you but cold; you're alone. This dark night of mine longs to call out your name, but she's lost her voice. She longs to call out to you and then find you and warm herself against your body for just a moment and oh forget these hours that are the death of me, death of me. This night burns for you.

It wears me out.

If this night had wings, it would fly straight to you; gather you up as you lay sleeping and bring you safely home – and you'd wrap your arms around me without even waking.

This night has no words of wisdom to offer.

This night thinks only of you; dreams of you with eyes wide open; laments, and paces and paces its room. It is long, so long, so long. The night wants me to get some clothes on, get outside and look for him, but she knows that would be crazy, I mustn't do that, mustn't, can't. She wonders if there's anything left I *can* do. I could always join her, give myself to her – people do, she knows that, but she doesn't like the idea of flesh surrendering itself just out of despair. Flesh was meant for flesh, never for the abyss.

This dark night of mine loves you in the very depths of her heart, and in that darkness my love echoes hers.

This night hungers for every imagined morsel of sound; its eyes never leave me – they glide like moonlight, slide into every crevice; if you were only here, how she would caress you, so gently; so gently. This night aches for you.

This body waits for you.

This night wants to watch you as you come, you first, then me, both of us shaking with pleasure. This night wants to watch us gazing into each other's eyes, she wants every look to be a lover's. She wants to feel you jump between her hands… oh she would make herself so sweet, so sweet… This dark night of mine bites her lip when she thinks of you.

This night is long, it's long, so long; she will die with losing you, and take me with her.

Her search has no end.
She howls and rends her veil;
No longer can she hold her tongue,
But nowhere can she find you.

I miss you more and more.

Miss the sound of you.

The colour…

It is dawn; she becomes aware of the first light.

…it must be nearly morning…

From

CAMILLE
by Neil Bartlett

**(adapted from *La Dame aux camélias* by
Alexandre Dumas *fils*)**

Camille *opened at the Lyric Hammersmith, London, in
March 2003.*

Set in 19th century Paris, Camille follows the story of
MARGUERITE GAUTIER, otherwise known as *La Dame aux
camélias* in Alexandre Dumas' novel of the same name.
MARGUERITE is the most beautiful, glamorous and expensive
prostitute in town. Armand Duval falls in love with her on their
first meeting and, as Marguerite struggles with tuberculosis and
the thought of death, the obsession becomes mutual. They plan
to spend the summer together but Armand isn't happy that
MARGUERITE sees other men to pay her extensive debts. In this
speech, she explains her situation to him.

MARGUERITE

Young man either you have to love me less, or you have to try and understand me more.

I thought for a moment I was going to be happy. A whole summer with only one lover – imagine – a whole summer – but no, you needed to know how I was going to pay for it. Was it really so hard to guess?

– Oh, I know, I could have asked you; you are in love with me, after all; you could have got hold of at least twenty thousand somehow – your allowance from your Father is what, eight, ten thousand a year? But then there would always be the possibility that you'd blame me later on for making you spend it, and I don't want to owe you anything.

We're different to other women. *We don't own ourselves.* And in consequence of that we want things we can't have, we make love to people we shouldn't; and we make an art and an entertainment out of giving ourselves away. Sometimes men ruin themselves, ruin their entire lives for us, and they get nothing; sometimes they can have the lot for the price of a decent bunch of flowers. Not knowing which it's going to be is the only thing that can still make us laugh.

Sometimes of course we just feel like it and give ourselves away for absolutely nothing. I let you, for instance, have me quicker than I've ever let any other man – no, really – why? Because when you saw me with blood running down my chin you felt sorry for me. Because I think you are the only human being who ever has.

The only thing I ever wanted was a man who'd never ask me any questions. And then I met you. And you, you were young. Young enough for me to fall in love with the man I thought I might just be able to turn you into. The man I'd been looking for to come and fill up my very noisy and very crowded and very empty life. But you don't want the job; you think it's beneath you. You're as ordinary as every other man I've ever met.

So now do what the others do. Pay me, and never speak to me again.

MARGUERITE coughs.

From

GUARDIANS
by Peter Morris

Guardians *premiered in August 2005 on the Edinburgh Fringe, and received a 2005 Fringe First Award. The play was staged at the Pleasance Cavern by the Mahwaff Theatre Company.*

Guardians presents a series of alternating monologues by two characters called The English Boy and THE AMERICAN GIRL, who present their stories directly to the audience. The common thread through both sets of speeches is a series of photos depicting Iraqi prisoner abuse. THE AMERICAN GIRL grew up in an abusive home in rural West Virginia, joined the U.S. army to escape and was sent to Iraq where she was given the job of guarding Iraqi prisoners. She became involved in a violent, sexual relationship with her superior officer, which led to her participation in a series of photos involving prisoner abuse. She ends up in a military jail, where she relates her story to the audience. THE AMERICAN GIRL is a fictional character although she is based on the story of Lynndie England and the Abu Ghraib photos.

THE AMERICAN GIRL

Prolly the first thing they teach you, growing up in West
Virginia, is that our state is the marble capital of the world.

Not *marble* marble, like the stuff they make statues and stuff
out of, like the, uh, Washington Monument or whatever.
But marbles. The, uh, glass-beady round things that kids are
essposed to play with? I'm not real sure how ya play. It's like,
ya draw a circle in the sand. And ya knock somebody else's
out. And if ya knock it out, ya keep it.

I *think* that's the rules, but it tells ya something that I don't
really know how to play. 'Cause the kids who play good, play
for keeps, they're competitive types. They're goin places.
They're gonna grow up, go to college, and be rich. And we
don't get that type in West Virginia. Maybe ya get a glimpse
a one, but blink and the fucker's gone. Town I'm from's the
kinda place you drive through quick on your way to someplace
else. Pittsburgh thatta way, couple hours drive in the other
direction you find yourself in Philadelphia, Baltimore –

Washington, DC.

And yeah, funny thing is, now they're talking 'bout me down
there. Little old me. I can't think of anybody else from West
Virginia gets talked about down there. I mean, yeah, we got
some famous people, like Loretta Lynn and – well, Loretta
Lynn, mainly. And, uh, Chuck Yeager. Guy broke the sound
barrier? Which like my momma useta say, just tells ya how
fast anybody with a brain wants to get out.

Lord knows I did. So I did what ya do, signed up and joined
the army, spring of 2000. And for shit-sure I wasn't counting
on being sent anyplace. I mean, not anyplace that's a theater
of operations. And least of all god-fucking-forsaken towelhead
Eye-raq.

From

THE EUROPEANS
by Howard Barker

The Europeans *was first performed in 1993 on a UK tour by the Wrestling School, a theatre company that is committed to exploring the plays of Howard Barker.*

The Europeans is set in seventeenth century Austria, where war has ended with the Turks. During the siege of Vienna, KATRIN was raped by soldiers and had her breasts cut off. We meet her in a convent, where she is explaining her ordeal to one of the nuns.

KATRIN

In my own words.

Pause.

Words of my own.

Pause.

The poor have neither words nor drawers.

Pause.

Oh, for literacy, oh, for numeracy, oh, for any pack of lies!

Pause.

So the four soldiers said –

Pause.

No.
No. There may not have been four. And they may not have been soldiers. But they did have weapons and the Turk does not wear uniform so for the sake of.

Pause.

Let's say four.

Pause.

The four soldiers said lie down – well, they didn't say it, no, they did not say the words they indicated by very simple gestures this was expected of me, words were dispensed with, words were superfluous though much language was expressed on either side, by me, by them, but words not really, no.

Pause.

Consequently I lay my face down in the relatively sympathetic grass. OF COURSE I AM NOT IN THE LEAST ASHAMED DESCRIPTION COMES EASILY TO ME but can I have a glass of water? The dryness of my mouth suggests anxiety but I have had a dry mouth since my throat was cut, some channel or some duct was severed, something irreparable and anatomical.

A NUN places a glass of water by the chair and withdraws.

It's you who are ashamed not me but I forgive in all directions then one of them threw up my skirt excuse me –

She drinks.

Or several of them, from now on I talk of them as plural, as many-headed, as many-legged and a mass of mouths and of course I had no drawers, to be precise –

Pause.

I owned a pair but for special occasions. This was indeed special but on rising in the morning I was not aware of it, and I thought many things, but first I thought – no, I exaggerate, I claim to know the order of my thoughts WHAT A PREPOSTEROUS CLAIM – strike that out, no, among the CASCADE OF IMPRESSIONS – that's better – that's accurate – cascade of impressions – came the idea at least I DID NOT HAVE TO KISS.

Pause.

The lips being holy, the lips being sacred, the orifice from which I uttered my most perfect and religious thoughts only the grass would smear them but no.

Pause.

Can you keep up? Sometimes I find a flow and then the words go – torrent – cascade – cascade again, I used that word just now! I like that word now I have discovered it, I shall use it, probably ad nauseam, cascading! But you –

Pause.

And then they turned me over like a side of beef, the way the butcher flings the carcass, not without a certain familiarity, coarse-handling but with the very vaguest element of warmth, oh, no, the words are going, that isn't what I meant at all, precision is so – precision slips even as you reach for it, goes out of grasp and I was flung over and this MANY MOUTHED THING –

She shudders as if taken by a fit, emitting an appalling cry and sending the water flying. The NUN *supports her. She recovers.*

Now I've spilled the water – don't say there's more where that came from – so it is with life – don't mop the floor, I can take it from the floor, so my mouth –

Pause. The NUN *withdraws.*

My mouth which I had held to be the very shape and seat of intimacy they smothered with wet and fluid – I don't think you could call them kisses – YES, YES, KISSES, THEY WERE KISSES I try to hide behind the language, oh, the language I do twist like bars of brass to shelter in, no, they were kisses because a kiss can be made of hatred – kisses, yes, oh, yes…

Pause.

They soaked, they drenched, they swilled me with their kisses, and bruised my lips and bit my mouth and thrust these thousand tongues into my throat AND THIS WAS ONLY THE BEGINNING ONLY THE BEGINNING YOU WITH THE BOOK AND PENCIL WAIT!

From

INCARCERATOR
by Torben Betts

Incarcerator *was first performed at The White Bear Theatre, London in September 1999.*

Written in rhyming couplets, which drive the drama forward to its bloody end, *Incarcerator* explores the lives of characters who find themselves trapped by their needs, wants and desires. This speech takes place when SMITH and Jessop are on their honeymoon and SMITH feels on top of the world.

SMITH

I love to lie upon a beach,
A dry white wine within my reach,
The sound of surf, the seagulls' swoop,
They dive and twist then loop the loop,
The sun's caresses, sand in toes,
This happiness just grows and grows!
I'm loved, I'm worshipped, I'm alive!
How other women can survive
Without the blessings I enjoy,
Without the house, the wheels, the boy,
Is quite beyond imagination,
Their lives sad puddles of stagnation:
No legs to flaunt, no looks to show,
No admiration…ever! No
Heads that turn in pubs and bars,
No lusty horns from pricks in cars,
No clothes, no flowers raining down,
No jewellery, no wedding gown,
No sex laid on when it's required,
The Gravebound they, the Undesired!
Poor wretched creatures! Suffragettes!
They boil and stew in their regrets,
As envy curdles through their veins,
They hiss and scratch and start campaigns,
Their passions always unrequited,
The Uninvolved, the Uninvited!
But me, Sweet Me, I'm full of lust!
My lover, though, is fit to bust…
I've fucked him raw and sucked him dry,
He must replenish his supply,
I've chewed his tongue and drunk his spit,
We celebrate desire! Submit

Us, therefore, if you will
To flaccid censure for until
That day our passion's spent
We'll fuck and fuck and fuck! Cement
Our marriage with this yearning,
And bollocks to your books and learning!
(*Rising.*) And now…I stand, this randy bitch!
One thing alone can soothe my itch!
(*Kicks* JESSOP.) Arise, arise…your damsel calls!
See where my good sir knight still spralls!
A naked duel, a clotheless bout
Is on the slab!

From

THE WAR NEXT DOOR
by Tamsin Oglesby

The War Next Door *was first performed at the Tricycle Theatre in February 2007.*

Max and Soph find themselves living next door to a wife beater, Ali, and his oppressed wife, HANA, who are middle-eastern immigrants. Max and Soph believe they're open-minded but the question of whether they should intervene or not creates an uncomfortable debate between them. In this speech, we find out how HANA truly feels. She is alone and speaks to the audience.

HANA

If I were a house
I'd be fallen down
windows all broke
holes in the floor
roof half off
so much dust it make you choke
no front door.

I need a place to hide
and I seen one just like it
near where I catch the number twenty-three
so I go inside
reminds me of me
place is fulla rotten wood
and rubbish
bugs crawling everywhere
smells bad, like fish;
don't bother me
it feels good.

There int no proper walls
ceiling's low
and full of holes
must be a bed up there cos I can see a pillow,
but you can't get up there
cos they's only half a stair.

Then I see a mouse
and I don't like mice
I says come here mousey
(I'm good at that
pretending to be nice)
but he run off

– he might of bin a rat –
jus as well he did
if he'd a come nearer
I'd of squashed the bastard flat.

Don't want no one in my home
not even a mouse
like I said
just want to be left alone
with stuff what's empty, broken, dead;
it's me it is, this house.

I like the dirt
I like the dark
If no one can see me I in't nobody's wife
and I forget to hurt
I like to hear nothing but the sound of my own breath
I like to hide
I don't believe in life
but I know there's somethin after death
cos I already died.

From

TALKING TO TERRORISTS
by Robin Soans

Talking to Terrorists *was commissioned by the Royal Court Theatre and Out of Joint Theatre Company. It was first performed at the Theatre Royal, Bury St Edmonds in April 2005.*

Talking to Terrorists portrays ordinary (real) people who have been involved in extraordinary events, including terrorists, hostages, survivors, politicians, journalists and psychologists. The writer, director and actors interviewed people from around the world who had been involved in or affected by terrorism. They met a woman who had joined the National Resistance Army in Uganda at the age of eight after leaving home when her father nearly beat her to death. She became a child soldier and took part in countless murders and tortures. This is the story of how she came to be on the run. She is speaking to an unseen interviewer. At the end of the play we learn that she is now 28 years of age and living in Denmark.

N.R.A.

One time…I was eight years old…my stepmother said, 'I'm going out, you had better cook the dinner.' I thought how the beef stew looked when she made it. I put nearly half a kilo of cream into the sauce and some curry; it had the right colour…it looked as it should. My stepmother told me to take it to the dining-table. My father, he sat there and shouted, 'Woman, is this the food you have prepared?' My stepmother said, 'Ask your daughter, she cooked the food. No one asked her to, but there it is.' My father, he told my brother, 'Go and get me chillies.' My father put all, every one, into the food, stirred it round and told me, 'You eat it now.' I thought, 'He's going to beat me anyway,' so I just sat there. He shouted at me, ordering me to eat. I still sat there, looking down. He told my brother to fetch a stick…the big stick for beating cows…he told me to lie down. I put my hands on my bum to protect me; he busted my fingers. He never cared if I died or not. I wished to die so the police would arrest him. He beat me on the head…I've still got something, look. Then he jammed my head between his legs, gripped tight, couldn't breathe, beating me, beating me…my stepmother moving the chairs so he could beat me more easily…my brothers and sisters screaming, 'Stop, stop…father, you're killing her…stop, stop…'

Silence. She passes her thumb across her forehead several times.

Eyes close. Tears.

When my father finished, I was full of blood.

It was the last day of school. Sofia, my best friend, came running, 'Don't go home…I heard your father's going to beat you again.' She took me to her house. I showed her mother my busted fingers. I said, 'If you send me home I will drink

Belmeth…it's what they put in the dip when they treat the animals.' I stayed with her that night. The next morning she showed me a photograph of my real mother and told me the journey to find her. I got on a bus. I left home. I was eight.

From

JAMAICA INN
by Daphne du Maurier in a new adaptation by Lisa Evans

Jamaica Inn *was commissioned by Salisbury Playhouse and first performed there in April 2004.*

Based on the classic novel by Daphne du Maurier, which is set in nineteenth century Cornwall, *Jamaica Inn* tells the story of MARY YELLAN who goes to live with fretful Aunt Patience and her oppressive husband, Joss, at Jamaica Inn on bleak Bodmin Moor. MARY's mother has just died so she has nowhere else to turn. She soon discovers mysterious things happening under the cover of darkness but it isn't until her uncle drinks a little too much one night that she discovers the awful truth. Joss is a 'wrecker' who lures ships aground on the Cornish coast, murders the people on board and steals their cargo. Not long after MARY is forced to watch the wreckers at work. She is tied, bound around her torso and pulled along either side by ropes.

MARY

It takes an eternity to reach the coast. The carriage is full of
men, my uncle beside me his elbow sharp in my side, the
smell of their bodies, of tobacco and stale drink. Their faces
swim up in a sea of smoke.

They're dragging me from the carriage. I smell salt on the air,
rain on my hand. I can hear the thunder and crash, the roar of
surf upon shingle. I don't remember then. It's dark. Sand on
my cheek. Voices far off. They've left me. I'm alone. I have
to escape. I'm stumbling along a ditch, away from the sea. It's
dark and my hair whips my eyes so I don't see him, crouched
waiting for me.

Then he's on me with his broken teeth and lips inches from
my face, crushing me. His hands are tearing at my skirts,
forcing me.

I'm bringing my head up fast. I catch him a blow to the chin
and his teeth trap his tongue. He's squealing like a rabbit.
His blood raining down on me. My fingers are in his eyes.
Gouging. His breath hot, sour in my face. His fingers clutching
at me. I'm not going to die here. I'm kicking him again and
again, a soft yielding like dough, and then I'm running. I can't
see. The fog is rolling in, and he's behind me somewhere. Any
second his hands on my throat.

I don't know what to do! I'm crawling. Down. There's a gap
in the mist. It's the shore. No! I've come too far. And there
they are, spread out in a thin line like black crows against the
white beach. Waiting. It's so quiet. Just the sound of the sea
breaking in rhythm on the shore. (*She looks sharply to one
side.*)

A light, high on the cliffs. Swinging, beckoning.

It's their light! Theirs! A figure beside it runs down, shingle
slipping, pointing towards the sea. Look there, the shadowed
hull, black spars like fingers spreading above it, dipping
and rising with the waves, searching through the mist. It's
coming closer like a moth to a candle. Two white eyes in the
darkness. Stop! Go back! It's hopeless, they can't hear me.
I'm caught. Hands across my mouth, bound, helpless. My
voice comes back to me on the wind and the night's full of
cries, of shattering groaning timber, and bones and the sounds
of sounds of…

Of fear. The tide's rushing in and I'm going to drown too.
(*Screams.*) No!

From

THE BOGUS WOMAN
by Kay Adshead

Commissioned by the Red Room, The Bogus Woman *was first performed as a work in progress at Waterman's Arts Centre in June 2000. The play premiered at the Traverse Theatre, Edinburgh in August 2000 and was subsequently performed at The Bush Theatre, London, in February 2001.*

This play presents the story of a young African journalist who is raped and her family murdered because of her writing. She flees to England with false documents and is detained at Campsfield and Tinsley House asylum centres, suffering indignities and torment at the hands of government officials and guards. Here, she tries to explain to an immigration officer why she felt it was necessary to seek asylum in England.

YOUNG WOMAN

to make ends meet
while my husband studied

I worked as a journalist
for eight and a half months
three days a week.
On February ninth
I received a note
posted to the office
where I worked.

It wasn't signed.
I wasn't scared.

Journalists
who wrote
on issues
concerning
human rights

routinely
received threats

but

words are bullets
And one day
from me
perhaps
a careless spray.

A careless spray.

As I say
March first nineteen ninety-seven

was a happy day!

This is what happened
on March second.

Soldiers were they?

My sister at the table
a copy of last months Vogue
got from the shop.

She is drawing
the seasons dresses,
colouring them in
with a kids pencil crayon set.

Red being the year's black.

Just before,
they kicked in the door

and shot off her face,

because they hadn't liked
the words I'd written

she smudged one line
with a small wet finger,
excited,
at getting it
exactly right.
   She screams.
No No No. Not her, not her!
No, Me! ME! ME!

My husband
in front of me

stopped the bullets
for a while
then died I think,
without a sound.

My father springs
he speaks in tongues.

His madness makes them stop.
And –
for just a half second,
of a second,
their jaws drop.

Strong magic
has made him
three men's height
and strength.
Then
they plunge their bayonets
in him,
without hate
it seems,
the swift jabs
and light steps
as delicate
and dainty
as a dance.

The tall one's
bayonet

pierces the linoleum,
sticks in
and breaks.

He curses

Pulling it out of my father's neck
he tries to fix it back
on his rifle.
He can't.
He seems put out.

A single bullet
through one eye
stops the horror
for my mother.

> *YOUNG WOMAN starts to edge back panting, whimpering. She
> is terrified.*

> *The mewl of the new born baby.*

(*Very softly.*) My baby,
oh my baby,
please, please,
my baby, my baby…

PART THREE:
THIRTIES

From

SLEEPING DOGS
by Philip Osment

Sleeping Dogs *was first performed in September 1993 by Red Ladder Theatre Company.*

Sleeping Dogs explores the tensions between Christians and Muslims during the war in the former Yugoslavia. Trouble has reached a small town in the south of the country, where Christians and Muslims have peacefully co-existed for some time. The children of the town are sent away to safety but their bus is stopped by Christian militiamen and the Muslim children are murdered. SABINA, a Muslim woman in her thirties, sent her daughter on that bus. Here, she holds her dead child and speaks to her female neighbours: Irma, Nadja and Hamida.

SABINA

Still warm,
She's still warm.
While I was measuring out the flour
She was sitting chatting to her friend.
While I was weighing out the butter,
Armed men stepped in front of the bus.
While I was mixing them together,
They shot the driver and got on board.
While I was adding sugar
They separated my daughter from her friend
Lined her up with the other Muslims on the bridge.
While I was cracking eggs
Someone held a knife to her neck.
While I was stirring them in,
He slit her throat.
As I poured the mixture into the tin
She died.
Feel her,
She's still warm.

She drops the knife to the ground.

They go to comfort her.

Leave me.

From

ONCE WE WERE MOTHERS
by Lisa Evans

Once We Were Mothers *was first performed at the New Vic Theatre, Newcastle-under-Lyme in September 2004.*

This play interweaves the stories of three mothers who all experience joy and suffer heartbreak but in very different situations. MILENA is a Bosnian Muslim in the 1990s and her world is shattered by the civil war. Here she describes how her best friend, Nevenka, was killed by Serb soldiers whilst her daughter survived.

MILENA

A long time later my daughter told me how they came to our
flat. Nevenka was playing with the children while I was out
searching for food. If only I hadn't gone out that morning. If
only we had made do with what we had. But we had nothing
so I left them. They were herded onto a bus. My daughter
remembered the number as having two digits, then driven for
what seemed to her like hours, the women trying to keep the
children calm, Nevenka all the way telling them funny stories
about when they were little. They had no food or water, only
a small carton of juice my mother in law shoved into their
hands as they left, which they shared, sitting on the back seat
of the bus. As I hear this story I imagine my children's faces
looking back through the window searching for a last glimpse
of home, of something familiar, of their childhood. As it was
told to me next a convoy of jeeps drives past, the bus pulls
off the road, rolls down towards the river, branches snapping
against the windows and halts. Men are firing their guns into
the air. Children are screaming. A radio crackles orders. The
shriek of river birds as they rise off the water in flight. Then
orders. Out of the bus, pushed and jostled, elbows and fists,
stumbling into the air, Faruk falls against one of the soldiers
who brings the heel of his rifle down onto my son's skull.
He crumples like tissue. Nevenka turns. He is gone. She is
pushed, my daughter beside her, to the brink of the water,
hands on heads, and the women stand poised, elbows like
wings, the river lapping the hems of their coats and then
they rise and run and fall in a spatter of bullets. Some only
wounded running into the water as if they could rise like the
geese into the air and away. And my daughter sees Nevenka's
coat beside her, whispy red ribbons trailing from it. And in the
coat is Nevenka who is dead, face down in a river of blood.
And my daughter falls too, falls and dives down into the red

brown water like a frog with a heron at its back, expecting
at any moment the sharp beak to snap her spine. She swam.
Not for her country, not for Yugoslavia, that was lost. But for
herself, for survival.

She stayed underwater, till her lungs swelled and the blood
vessels were ready to burst through her eyes, while up above
her guns spat rage till every movement in the water ceased.
And then she did a remarkable thing as only those in danger of
extinction will do when fear slows time. She opened her eyes,
as if to see the world once more before she was swallowed
by the river, and she saw amongst the debris floating above
her on the surface of the water, an empty juice carton, and
she smiled remembering the one they had shared in the
back seat of the bus a lifetime ago when Nevenka told them
happy stories. For what seemed like hours she lay submerged
beneath the flotsam of the river and breathed life through
a paper straw and only when darkness fell like a merciful
curtain across another bloodstained day, did she dare to raise
her head out of the water, and finding she was alone, drag
herself up the bank.

From

THE DARKER FACE OF THE EARTH
by Rita Dove

The Darker Face of the Earth, *by the former US Poet Laureate, was first performed at the Oregon Shakespeare Festival in Ashland, Oregon, USA in July 1996 and in the United Kingdom at the Royal National Theatre in August 1999.*

The Darker Face of the Earth is an updated version of the Oedipus story but set on a plantation in South Carolina in the 1840s. PHEBE was born a slave on the plantation and is in her early teens when the play opens. However, twenty years pass and she finds herself caught up with the revolutionary ideas of a charismatic new slave, Augustus Newcastle. Here, she explains her mother's death to him.

PHEBE

Mama worked in the kitchen until
I was about five; that's when
fever broke out in the quarters.
She used to set table scraps out
for the field hands, and I
stuck wildflowers in the baskets
to pretty 'em up. Mama said
you never know what a flower can mean
to somebody in misery.
That fever tore through the cabins like wildfire.
Massa Jennings said the field hands
spread contamination and forbid them
to come up to the house, but
Mama couldn't stand watching them
just wasting away – so she started
sneaking food to the quarters at night.

Then the fever caught her, too.
She couldn't hide it long.
And Massa Jennings found out.

   Gulps a deep breath for strength, reliving the scene.

Mama started wailing right there at the stove.
Hadn't she been a good servant?
Who stayed up three nights straight
to keep Massa's baby girl among the living
when her own mother done left this world?
Who did he call when the fire
needed lighting? Who mended the pinafores
Miss Amalia was forever snagging on bushes?

Mama dropped to her knees
and stretched out her arms along the floor.

She didn't have nowheres to go;
she'd always been at the Big House.
"Where am I gonna lay
my poor sick head?" she asked.

He stood there, staring
like she was a rut in the road,
and he was trying to figure out
how to get round it.
Then he straightened his waistcoat
and said: "You have put me and my child
in the path of mortal danger,
and you dare ask me what to do
with your nappy black head?"
He didn't even look at her –
just spoke off into the air
like she was already a ghost.

   Woodenly.

She died soon after.

From

TAKING CARE OF BABY
by Dennis Kelly

Taking Care of Baby *was first performed at Birmingham Repertory Theatre in May 2007.*

This is the story of DONNA MCAULIFFE, imprisoned for murdering her two infant children. The play is structured like a documentary with a series of probing interviews. DONNA was eventually released from prison and now recalls her first night there for the reporter.

DONNA

And so I'm, erm, just erm, standing there, standing there and this girl, there's this girl lying on the top bunk and she's not saying – she had thinning hair on one side, alopecia, I think it was – and she's not saying a word, she's just staring at the ceiling and I was too scared to move really, so I just stood there, I mean, and the door's, erm, closed, just closed behind me and I'm, erm, you know, in this cell with this girl and she's not – do you want all this?

Beat.

and she's not looking, she's not looking at me.

So I just put my stuff on the, er, er, I put it on the er, bottom bunk, I was gonna put it on, erm, on the er, cupboards, shelf drawers, I was going to put it in the drawers but I didn't know which were hers and I didn't want to, I didn't want to open them or anything.

Oh yeah, and there were people in, erm, on the landing, I mean in the other cells on the landing, women, I mean, and they were like hissing and sometimes calling, you know, things… You know, killer, er, murderer, bitch…you murderer, you bitch, you murdering bitch, we're going to kill you you murdering bitch…cunt, things like that. And I just lay, I just lay on my bunk with my things there around me because I was too scared to, I didn't even take my shoes off actually, I was still wearing my shoes, but I was like that for about forty minutes and then this girl, the girl above me, er she suddenly spoke and she had this, I think she was either from the, either from Wales or the West country because her accent was quite, it was a mixture, or, but I couldn't tell and she said, erm, she said 'Don't speak' she said, erm, 'Don't speak because I'm trying not to hurt you. I've got six months left so I'm trying not to hurt you, so if you make me hurt you, I'm really, really gonna fucking hurt you.'

Beat.

And, and she meant it as well. She was really trying her hardest not to hurt me. I mean not for me, for her, you know.

Silence.

And, erm, then she erm, she kept saying what she was going to do if I made her hurt me and it was like, it was like cutting my eyes and stamping on my stomach and my face and putting bleach in my eyes after she'd cut the er, sliced the er, made a cut in, sliced the er, eyeball and things, it was a lot about the eyes, actually, she concentrated a lot about, on and around the eyes and that went on for about two hours.

Beat.

That was my first night in prison.

From

VICTORY AT THE DIRT PALACE
by Adriano Shaplin

Victory at the Dirt Palace, *a Riot Group production, was first performed at La Val's Subterranean Theater, Berkeley, California in July 2002. It subsequently opened at the Edinburgh Fringe Festival in August 2002, where it received the Scotsman Fringe First Award and the Herald Angel Award. In January 2003, Victory at the Dirt Palace opened at Riverside Studios, London.*

Victory at the Dirt Palace takes place in two American television news studios: James Mann and K MANN (Katherine) are father and daughter, employed by competing networks as prime time news broadcasters. This monologue is situated towards the end of the play. K MANN's new rival, Andrew, has just shown pictures of her engaged in sexual acts on national television. These were given to Andrew by Spence, K MANN's assistant and former lover. In the original monologue K MANN is banging Spence's head onto the news broadcast desk as she attempts to explain herself to the nation on camera, however, this can be easily changed by the actor, if the speech is being presented solo.

K MANN

What happened? Where did he get those photos? Where did those photos come from? Am I dreaming? Is this a fucking nightmare?

(*Grabbing* SPENCE.) Where did he get those photos?

YOU????

(*Grabs* SPENCE *by the throat and slams his head onto the desk, holding it there with her hands.*) You think I'm scared of you, you little weasel? (*Looking at the audience.*) Go ahead, turn my camera on, I'm ready to go. Turn it on. When I'm done with you you'll be interning for NO PAY. You'll be licking twat for pennies! You'll be sucking ass for dollars! You'll be knocking boots with flip-flops.

> *K's Nightly News Broadcast music swells.* SPENCE *is still pinned to the desk by K, trying not to be noticed.*

Okay, I'm on? Yes? Good evening ladies and gentlemen. I'm K Mann. New developments in the aftermath of the tragic events of 24-hours ago, but first: No doubt you've just seen photographs of me displayed on national television. These are private photos of private moments, ripped from their intimate context and revealed, no doubt, to tarnish my reputation. This is a desperate, obscene act of sabotage, perpetrated by adolescent hucksters and JEALOUS (*Banging* SPENCE's *head for emphasis.*) snivelling middlemen with all the warmth of an extinguished effigy. I am confident, VERY CONFIDENT, that the American people will not be fooled by this calculated insult to their intelligence. I am confident that the viewing public, and my employer the SAL New Organisation, will neither judge *nor punish* me for taking pleasure in the geometry of my temporary flesh. What?

K presses her ear-piece. She is receiving a message from the control room.

Oh, I'm fired? WELL FUCK YOU. I QUIT!

From

13 OBJECTS
(South of that Place Near)
by Howard Barker

13 Objects, *directed by Howard Barker, opened at the Birmingham Rep in October 2003.*

A collection of thirteen short self-contained plays explore how people make emotional (and sometimes disturbing) investments in inanimate objects. In *South of that Place Near* we find a woman with a postcard from her lover. He has asked her to join him but the address on the postcard has been smudged and she has no way of knowing where to find him.

WOMAN

A WOMAN *holding a postcard.*

The post office
The trickery of the post office
The trickery and malevolence of the post office
The trickery malevolence and criminal mismanagement of the
post office
Is legendary is it not
THEY DELIBERATELY CONCEAL THE ORIGINS OF
LETTERS
How can they in an age of such sophisticated and sensitive
machinery contrive to
SMUDGE THE CANCELLATION MARK
It's deliberate
Oh yes
It's human intervention
Some clerk read this some sorter I don't know some minor I
don't know some operative at the very lowest levels read it
bored perhaps thought oh a postcard I'll read that stopped
the machine oh yes they can be stopped trod on a button
stopped it paused and read squinting short-sighted put his
glasses on read my read his the few untidy words and thought
I'll smudge I'll cause the name of this place to be rendered
utterly illegible not just difficult but utterly oh utterly he
must have smiled he must have known and smiled at my
inevitable frustration laughing loud triumphant smudging card
from nowhere
JOIN ME
JOIN ME
SAYS MY LOVE

Pause.

Picture of a mountain and a cable car and underneath the
legend the mountain and the cable car as if it wasn't obvious

but I don't criticize I keep my passionate resentment for those
who most deserve it
HOW MANY MOUNTAINS
SNOW-CAPPED MOUNTAINS
HOW MANY SNOW-CAPPED MOUNTAINS HAVE A
CABLE CAR
And it's antique
The card
Typically he sent an antique card black and white or grey to be
precise no brilliant colour splashed with names of the resorts
no discreet ever discreet the mountain and the cable car the
stamp is Swiss that helps ha a Swiss mountain with a cable
car ha and even if the mountain has not changed the cable car
certainly has
JOIN ME
JOIN ME
Oh I want to
Oh I so want

From

PICASSO'S WOMEN
by Brian McAvera

The first four monologues from Picasso's Women *were broadcast on BBC Radio 3 in May 1996. The full text was first staged at the National Theatre, London in July 2000.*

Picasso's Women is a series of eight monologues, in which the lovers, wives and muses of Picasso relate their stories after they have died. This speech is taken from the fifth monologue, spoken by MARIE-THÉRÈSE WALTER. She met Picasso when she was seventeen years old, while he was still married to Olga Khokhlova, the Russian ballet dancer. MARIE-THÉRÈSE became his lover and muse but never really understood much about art, preferring athletic pursuits. Eight years later she gave birth to Picasso's daughter, Maya. A year after Maya was born, Picasso fell in love with the artist, Dora Maar and lost interest in MARIE-THÉRÈSE. She hanged herself after Picasso died. Despite having died in her sixties, MARIE-THERESE returns here to speak to the audience at thirty-four years of age.

MARIE-THÉRÈSE

But I haven't told you how we met!

It was six months earlier, a cold day in January and I was standing in front of the Galeries Lafayette department store on the Boulevard Haussmann, waiting on a girlfriend. And there he was in his fine thick overcoat, staring at me. He even walked around me once or twice as if he couldn't believe his eyes.

(*She imitates his thick accent again.*) 'Miss. You have an interesting face. I would like to do your portrait. I am Picasso.'

Well *I* didn't know who he was, did I? That took him by surprise! He looked as if he couldn't *quite* believe it. But I wasn't interested in paintings.

Did I tell you that my father was a painter? No?
I never met my daddy. On my birth certificate it says 'Father unknown'.
Mummy liked paintings, and she played classical music on the piano and read classical literature but I never bothered with any of that. Now gymnastics, that I do enjoy – but I'm forgetting, aren't I!

He simply grabbed me by the arm and asked if I'd like breakfast.
I was hungry, and it was free so I had a plate of bacon and eggs, a whole basket of rolls, and four cups of coffee. Well, what use is a croissant to a gymnast?

And he was so amazed that he asked me if I was English as he'd never seen anyone other than the English or the Americans eating like that so early in the morning. Poor dear! He was such a...a diabolical man...but I know he couldn't help it.
(*Brightly.*) We met two days later at Saint-Lazare metro.

(*Giggles. Imitates his accent.*) 'We will do great things together.'
I'm afraid to say that I burst out laughing!

But wasn't he a foreigner, and a nice man, with a lovely thick accent like treacle.

He was wearing a blue serge suit, but he never could keep the creases. He always had things in his pockets, packets of cigarettes, small sketch books, matches, bits of crayon, pencils.
(*An odd piquant tone.*) And he had a white shirt with a red-and-black tie.
(*Brightly.*) I still have the tie!

And when he'd shove his hands into his coat pockets, searching for something, the tips of the fingers would be grubby with crayon dust and bits of tobacco.
He told me he was married but I didn't care. He had such beautiful blackcurrant eyes, and a thick, dark, shiny lock of hair that wandered over his forehead. And he was so… so stocky, proud, erect, he seemed to look at you and into you and all around you, and will you to do what he wanted and he had such powerful yet feminine hands.
You've understood me, haven't you?
A woman doesn't resist Picasso.
I did for six months. I was seventeen.
I knew nothing. I was innocent, a gamine, but it was *me* that he selected, me, out of the hundreds, the thousands who threw themselves at him.

From

FEVER
by Reza de Wet

Fever *was first produced by the Performing Arts Council of the Transvaal at the Windybrow Theatre in Johannesburg in March 1991 as* A Worm in the Bud.

South African playwright, Reza de Wet, tells the story of EMMA, a thirty year old English woman, who travels to the Cape Colony to teach the children of a Boer family in the 19th Century. The children's mother has died and the household is run by the father, Mr Brand, and his sister, Miss Brand. EMMA's story unfolds through correspondence with her sister, Katy, back in England, and, EMMA's diary entries that are spoken aloud by both EMMA and Katy. At the beginning of the play we learn that EMMA has died in the Colony so, when her trunk arrives back in England, Katy steals her diary to learn more. This speech is actually one of EMMA's diary entries towards the end of the play. Here, EMMA struggles with her sexual feelings towards Mr Brand.

EMMA

Past midnight. I awoke very suddenly. And then I realised…
that he was calling me… Drawing me to him… And we were
alone…alone in the house… I…rose like a…sleepwalker… I
could not…resist… I moved to my door…up the passage…
I could see the door to his room… It was slightly ajar. I
could not stop… I could not… I moved to the door… As I
was protesting…struggling…some other creature seemed
to…inhabit my body…to be driving me forward… I pushed
open his door… It was dark inside… I could smell him…
tobacco…and sweat…as dark as the abyss of depravity…
And then…with an almost superhuman strength…I stepped
back! Yes! I stepped back! In a moment I was running down
the passage and out – out into the garden. I ran blindly…
I could feel my hair…tumbling down my back… I fell and
tore my nightdress…but still I ran! To get away! To get away
from him! My breath rasped in my throat… A wind came
up…an ill wind… The air was full of cries… The evil…was
palpable…the sky seemed dark and veined…like the wings of
a large bat… (*Silence.*) At last I found myself in the graveyard.
I was seeking refuge…solace…among the souls of the
departed. I…fell to the ground. After a time…I realised that
I was lying near the grave…of the children's dear mother…
(*Gentle, romantic, transported.*) Oh, it reminded me of Mrs
Dante Gabriel Rossetti… Her flame-coloured hair… And
when…they opened her grave…to retrieve his poems…they
found that…her miraculous hair…had grown…filling the
coffin…with its radiance. And I thought of their mother…in
a similar shroud of shining hair… At the first hint of dawn…I
went back to the house… Evil is always banished by light…

From

A NEW YORK THREESOME: MANHATTAN BREAST COMPANY
by Lesley Ross

Manhattan Breast Company *was first performed at The Albany Theatre, Deptford in August 2004.*

This is the third monologue in a trilogy called *A New York Threesome* that focuses on three very different people and the impact they have on each other's lives: Sam, his wife BRONWEN and his gay brother Davey. *Manhattan Breast Company* is BRONWEN's story. BRONWEN is American and met her English husband in New York. She moved to England after they married but a car accident, in which she was driving, left him in a vegetable-like state. He has since died and her husband's brother, Davey, is looking after her daughter in England whilst she lives back in New York. At the beginning of the monologue we are told that B is in her thirties, staying in Paris and pregnant. We learn from the monologue that she came to Paris on a fact-finding mission – to find the 'perfect nipple'. She has been commissioned to design some t-shirts for drag queens in New York that have in-built breasts. Along the way she met Peter, who helped her to love again. This section of the monologue explains their first meeting just as she arrives in Paris. The entire monologue is spoken directly to the audience.

A note from the playwright: 'The symbol '/' indicates a change of thought without any pause whatsoever. The dialogue should continue to flow. Whereas '...' can be read as a moment of silence.

B

I did not sleep on the flight and there was no time for a shower at Heathrow and I'm on some tiny bucket plane to Paris and I'm pissed at the guy across the aisle who asks me questions as I sit down. I have no desire for conversation, thank you. Nice eyes kinda.

Sorta.

No, leave me alone. Thank God for the iPod / music soothes some of the flight over / smoothes over the chat / batteries let you down / batteries programmed to interfere with smooth ride / should have charged the batteries. Put the music away / coming into land / out of the seat / almost home dry / oh God, crash into / almost but not quite / almost crash into guy on the opposite aisle. Nice eyes.

'No, please, after you.'

But he insists I go first, so I do. My God, really nice eyes / get away from me. He's wearing a / was it red or pink?

(*To member of the audience.*) You prefer red or pink? Yeah, you. Red or pink? Okay, pink, red, either way it was vile, but he has beautiful eyes. Blue. Definitely blue. And shimmering. Like the ocean / no, more specific, like the water just off Rott Nest Island. Near Perth, Australia. Really blue. Oh, but then you've never been / so go, and then you'll get it. But blue or not, I am now aware that he's still there walking almost beside me but not / No sorta behind but enough to let me know that if I just turn my head slightly he'll be in my line of vision and he'll smile, maybe those beautiful eyes will sparkle at me. Fuck Off.

Okay, so I'm paranoid, but I've hardly slept in days and I don't want some slick euro guy coming in my face. Oh God…he was in my personal space.

No, don't stand next to me at the carousel / no, don't smile at me and pretend you think that's your bag. Oh, that is his bag / Don't smile at him he might not go. Why is he still there? How many bags does he need? No, that's my / get your filthy hands off my bag.

'Oh, thank you so much, but I think I'll manage it thanks. What? Oh, yeah, it is sorta heavy.'

Think.

'But at least it's just the one, hey.'

And can he not see it's on wheels? He wants to know what I'm doing in Paris. Why would I tell him?

'Oh, I'm just visiting a friend. And doing some work, too.' Oh why did I tell him I was working, please don't ask me about my work. Please don't show any interest in my work.

Beat.

Oh yeah, he's a guy, he doesn't. But he is visiting a friend, too. Great, and it's also his first time in Paris. Always fascinating.

'Well have a nice trip' / Life, I should have said life, have a nice life and get the hell out of mine.

From

I LIKE MINE WITH A KISS
by Georgia Fitch

I Like Mine With A Kiss *was premiered at The Bush Theatre, London in February 2007.*

ANNIE is a 39 year old single mother who lives in London. She accidentally became pregnant after casual sex with a friend and has been planning to have the baby despite what her mother, teenage daughter and best friend think. Unfortunately it just doesn't work out. Here, she explains to them exactly what happened.

A note from the playwright: 'Capitals denote emotional intensity rather than volume.'

ANNIE

Have felt rough all week, cramps and some bleeding, which I wanted…well you all didn't need to know about that. Even if you bleed a lot, that does not necessarily mean that you are going to have a miscarriage, pain is much more of a sign. I didn't want to ask anything of you all, so I kept it to myself… kept it to my… Yesterday I really didn't feel well all day. My body ached all over and I couldn't even lift a cup y'know…but I was like in tune with my heart. (*Beat.*) I looked out the window and thought…if ever there was a day to…end…this was it…this was going to be it. Yesterday I was aware I had a miscarriage…nature responded. A tad heartbreaking and rather ugly… As I stood up…held onto the sink, sorry that's how I broke your bubble bath Freya…well it then just trickled down my legs…wiped it and saw it on my hands…mixed IT with my tears…but I'm okay about it… I am… I am… I really am… Thought you all might be pleased. I know it's something you all wanted…something you all wished for…me…thought was for the best, although I believe we have all

In some ancient African tribe…well there is this myth, that when the women of the tribe all wanted a particular woman to miscarry, they somehow all got together and conspired to make it happen…spiritually like… (*Beat.*) I can pour a bottle of wine down my throat now and as my body is already getting back to normal and I am sure you would all like to celebrate. My mother, my daughter, my best friend… Let's have a little toast…a toast…to my…freedom? MY FREEDOM. It's all just waiting for me now isn't…all just there and waiting…life? COME ON THEN…MY LIFE…LIFE…COME ON…COME ON. CATCH ME WHILST YOU CAN LIFE…CATCH ME WHILST YOU CAN.

PART FOUR: FORTIES PLUS

From

LATER
by David Pownall

This play was first performed at The King's Head, Islington, London in June 1979.

Later is a monologue spoken by SONIA, a forty year old Russian woman who has been missing for sixteen years after the turmoil of the revolution. It is now 1937 and her family, in a small village near Novgorod, hold a séance to call her home. SONIA answers the call and explains to them how she died.

SONIA

It wasn't so bad after all. Imagination is a terrible thing and I
know what hell you must have gone through, but believe me,
Death isn't as bad as it's painted. I would rather have been
at home when it happened, however, here I am anyway. The
circumstances are different. I'm here, you're there, there's
this space in-between, but at least we're in touch again. Before
we go any further, I'm sorry. I should have told you. You
would have helped me, I know that. Going off on my own
to sort it out was stupid when I had you both to give a hand.
Having had time to think about it I can see that I was in too
much of a hurry, didn't want to waste time, didn't want the
burden of it right then when so much was happening in my
life, so I thought, get rid. Have it removed and do it sensibly,
practically, don't feel about it. Keep that for later. Now it
makes me smile. My life was half over and I was thinking of
later. When would I have had that child? And you were so
eager to be old, old grandparents. With everything that was
being torn up and changed around you, I sympathised with
that. It would have been an anchor for you. Instead, I went
to Petrograd. Selfish. Stupid. You would think that I had all
that great movement in my bones, that as I walked along the
street I shifted the world with me – it was absolutely selfish
and self-centred. I was one woman and the only thing I could
do to the required standard was work a sewing machine.
But they did look smart, my uniforms. I was in all of them,
wandering about, saluting, shouting. It was me looking out of
all the button-holes, and my mind was being stretched. It was
so exciting, even in that room in Novgorod with all the others,
measuring great men across the shoulders…

Pause

This will have to be kept a secret. Don't let anyone here talk
about what we're doing or there will be trouble. For one thing

the authorities won't accept the validity of this meeting, and for another they will accuse you all of promoting primitive superstition. Christianity is bad enough but this...

Pause

It took you long enough to get round to it. Not that I have been waiting for the call, but I knew you were desperate. Not knowing must have been the worst part of it. I gave a false name to the man who did it and when it happened to go wrong he just dumped me as best he could and said nothing. I disappeared. He stuck me and the baby, what there was of it into a tin box with a pile of bricks and slid us into the river. We're still there, the matter anyway.

From

SUFFERING THE WITCH
by David Foley

Suffering the Witch *was first performed as* American Witch *at the Théâtre de Poche, Brussels in October 2004, in the French translation by Sally Micaleff.*

Sharon left her home town, somewhere in the dusty Pentecostal American outback, at the age of sixteen. She has now returned, twelve years later, to face her troubled past. MURIEL is one of Sharon's mother's best friends. She is described as 'a pert and well-maintained forty'. This speech is set in the church hall, where there is a 'welcome home' party for Sharon. MURIEL addresses the audience but is constantly interrupted by other parishioners.

MURIEL

I tell you you could have knocked me over with a feather
when I first heard. Sharon's Daddy – Mel Driscoll – pillar of
the community – right-hand man to Pastor Michaels – had
taken liberties *with his own daughter!* Now you may say such
things are best kept in the family – (*To an unseen parishioner.*)
Hello! How are you? Nice to see you! – and you may be right.
I don't know. But when Sharon went to tell her Mama – Isn't
that a pretty dress? Is it new? Takes ten pounds right off you!
– when she went to tell her Mama, Happy just refused to
believe her. Said she must be possessed by demons. Said she
should pray and – Hello! – pray and ask Jesus to clean out
her mind. Well, you would have thought poor Sharon *was*
possessed from what happened next. Because one Sunday
at church, she just got up, I mean, Sharon just stood up and
screamed it out in front of everybody. And in such an awful
way. Like she couldn't help it. Like she *was* possessed. And
then she just passed out in a fit right there on the church
floor. – (*She mimes taking a cup of coffee from somebody.*)
For *me?* Aren't you sweet? Cream and two Sweet-n-Lows?
Now how do you remember something like that? Thank you!
– Of course, everyone was just *aghast*, and Sharon just lying
there, not quite asleep, but not really awake either. Eyes
open. Staring at nothing. Mouth moving and no sound coming
out. And no one knew what to do. It was like a demon just
come right into our church and took one of our own in front
of our very eyes. And Mel went all red and he was the first
to say it. "Demons," he said. "It's demons." – Oh, no, honey.
I'm watching my figure. Uh-uh. Not even one. – That was
the start of a real bad time. Well, the girl should-a been in a
hospital or something. But Happy and Mel just didn't know
what to do with her, so they just let her wander around. In
school, out of school, downtown, up to the mountains, out on

the highway, anywhere she pleased, and all the time looking so strange that you began to think, well, maybe she *wasn't* possessed. Maybe she was just *crazy*. – I think he's over there, sugar. Talking to Judy Gonzalez – Well, who knows what would have happened except it all got to be too much for Mel and he broke. He confessed to Pastor Michaels. Pastor made him confess to Happy. And in the end he made his confession to the whole church, sobbing and – Not now, honey – holding onto the hands of his wife and daughter. It was an awful sight. A terrible awful sight. The will and grace of God working among us, redeeming sin, calling a sinner back by this terrible ordeal of humiliation and redemption. We took him back in, of course. Forgave him as Jesus says to forgive. But if you ask me, it killed him in the end. Two years later he dropped down dead at his hardware store. Heart attack. But Sharon was long gone by then. She didn't even come back for the funeral. You can imagine what some folks thought about that!

From

LIFE AFTER LIFE
by Paul Jepson and Tony Parker

Life After Life *was first performed at the National Theatre Loft in London in May 2002.*

This play is a dramatic piece of reportage, which draws on interviews with murderers attempting to rebuild their lives. VALERIE has just done eleven years in prison after strangling her best friend; she is 41 years old and bitter about the opportunities available to her now that she has been released. The interview takes place in her council flat.

VALERIE

I saw an advert in a magazine for a live-in cook-housekeeper wanted for an elderly couple not far from here. I went along and the old couple were fine, I liked them and they seemed to like me too; they showed me where I'd have my own comfortable little bed-sitting room with a colour TV, my own kitchenette and toilet and everything, I couldn't believe my luck.

So I began the job. It was true the old lady could be a bit difficult at times if things weren't exactly as she liked them, but that was no strain for me, particularly after some of the types you meet in prison, I can tell you. And it was the old lady herself, before we even got to the end of the two-month trial period, who asked me if I'd stay on on a permanent basis.

But when I went back and told my probation officer about it, she absolutely took my breath away. She said if it was going to be permanent, I had to tell the daughter and her husband.

I rang the daughter up and said could I go round and see her. She was on her own when I got to her house; she invited me in and to sit down. I took a deep breath and then said, 'I'm under the supervision of a probation officer, and she insists that I have to give you some information.' She was very nice, she smiled, and she said well lots of people were on probation, what'd I done? I said no, I wasn't on probation, I was on parole. Like most people she didn't know the difference: she asked what did that mean? I said well I'd been in prison for a long time on a life sentence. And that was it, I had to say what for: that I'd committed a murder. I'd killed someone and I was only released on license.

Since then I've had a part-time job that lasted two weeks at a hamburger take-away, then I was off with a bad cold for four days and they told me not to bother going back; then a waitress for a week, and a barmaid for two nights that I walked out of because I hate pubs and men trying to chat you up and telling you dirty jokes all the time. Apart from that, nothing; and I live like I am now, on Social Security. The probation really wrecked things for me, that's what I feel. I had my own job, my own nice little place, I worked hard and put up with the old lady's funny little ways: and they completely fucked it all up.

From

FALLING
by Shelley Silas

The world premiere of Falling *took place at the Bush Theatre, London in November 2002.*

LINDA is forty-two years old and has been trying to get pregnant for the past seven years with her partner, Pete. They've just miscarried for the fifth time and she's thinking about giving up and getting on with the rest of her life, however painful that may be. Here, LINDA is talking to her sister Kate who has three children of her own.

LINDA

You can't understand what it feels like. To not be able to have something you want so much. To wake every day wishing you'd made different choices, that someone had told you, warned you that you can't have it all. That you never could. It's just not possible.

The other day in Sainsbury's, this woman started shouting at her kid, a baby, about a year old. Its dummy had fallen, slipped out of its mouth, you know, by accident. And the woman got hold of it and shoved it back in really hard. And then she lifted her hand up and her fingers slapped the side of its face. 'Don't do that,' she said. 'Don't do that.' And the baby giggled and smiled and the dummy started to slip again and I could see her hand going up. And I stared at her, like, 'what do you think you're doing?' And she looked at me and pulled back her hand and laughed and said, 'kids, you know what they're like.' (*Beat.*) Sometimes I'll stare at the garden and imagine kids, our kids, running around in the summer, bare feet dragging along the grass, sticky fingers and big toothy smiles. Or I'll see a heavily pregnant woman and want it to be me, want to know how it feels. To have that inside you. To be special, so people know you're growing something new inside you. To have a fuss made, to never be the same person again, to have a new identity, to be a mother, a mum. And it hurts. It hurts to know I'll never be that special. That my special time has run out.

From

A WOMAN IN WAITING
by Yael Farber and Thembi Mtshali-Jones

A Woman in Waiting *was written and created by Yael Farber in collaboration with Thembi Mtshali-Jones and premiered at the National Arts Festival in Grahamstown, South Africa, in 1999. It is published alongside of* Amajuba: Like Doves We Rise *and* He Left Quietly *in* Theatre as Witness *(three testimonial plays from South Africa which were created with and based on the lives of the casts performing them).*

In *A Woman in Waiting* the actress THEMBI MTSHALI explores her experiences as a black South African woman during the Apartheid regime. She grew up in a small village with her grandparents whilst her mother worked in the kitchens of Durban in order for the family to survive. THEMBI only saw her mother once a year at Christmas. Eventually, when THEMBI was old enough, her mother brought her to live in the townships of Durban so they could be closer. When THEMBI has her own baby, Phumzile, she too is forced to leave her with family in order to work with white South Africans. Here, she recollects for the audience, how she felt. She holds the figure of a white child, constructed from empty clothing.

THEMBI

This child was a job like any other. But when you spend every hour of the day together, it's impossible not to become attached to one another. Somewhere beyond the madams, the dirty washing, the backrooms, and bad wages…

Was a child that depended on you for everything! Just a child…

I have held many babies in my time. Who knows? I might have held one of you.

She takes a second child's figure from the smaller wooden crate she has been sitting on.

Some I cared for with my hands…

She takes out a third child.

And some I cared for with my heart. But at any moment, you could be told you were no longer needed. And so I would have to take my love, pack it away, and unpack it for the next child I cared for.

She takes a small boy figure by the hand.

20 YR THEMBI: Come Shaun. Don't you want to go to the park?

She leans down to listen to what the child says to her.

Of course I'll stay with you. I'm not going to leave you. I'll be with you all the time.

Now, don't run too fast.

The child falls. She picks him up and holds him with great tenderness.

Sorry Baby! Don't cry.

She places the boy – as if on a swing – and rocks him.

Sit here and hold on tight.

THEMBI: (*Addressing* PHUMZILE *in her mind, as she swings the small boy.*)

Wo-Hey Phumzi! I would wonder the whole week what you were doing at home. Were you finishing your food? Were you taking your bottle? Or was my sister Thandi still giving you her empty breast for comfort? I envied the little white children I cared for. They had everything…including me! Whenever I played games with them, I would wish you were here too. But you were playing on the dusty streets of Kwamashu.

(*To the audience.*) By the end of the week – the waiting was the worst. Waiting for the family to finish dinner, so I could clear the table…

20 YR THEMBI: (*Collecting a dish.*) Thank you Master.

THEMBI: Wash up and finally go home to my child.

Waiting for the child to fall asleep in the evenings when her parents were out…

20 YR THEMBI: (*Holding the child, rocking her to sleep.*) Ssssh. I'm just going to the kitchen. I'll leave the door open.

OK, sssh! Don't worry. I'll stay here with you.

The phone rings.

Yes Madam… She's falling asleep…

(*Distressed.*) You're going to be late? What time?

But it's Friday. I'm supposed to go home tonight.

I'll miss my nine o'clock bus… I…but…

(*Resigned.*) OK, madam – I'll wait.

She puts down the phone and whispers to the child who has woken and is now crying for its mother.

It's OK, baby… Don't cry. Mummy's coming home soon.

THEMBI: (*To PHUMZILE in her mind.*) I'm coming home soon Phumzi.

Please wait for me if you can. I'm coming soon.

From

THE UNCONQUERED
by Torben Betts

The Unconquered *was first performed at the Byre Theatre of St Andrews, Scotland in February 2007.*

The country is in political turmoil over a people's revolution. One family's domesticity is dislocated and disturbed when starvation threatens and a mercenary soldier storms into the home and rapes the daughter. The girl tries to explain the horror of what she has experienced to her MOTHER and threatens to kill herself. Instead of trying to comfort her, the MOTHER reveals some of her own unhappiness.

MOTHER

Last night…last night, your father struck me. It was the first time. But it was my fault. I tend to annoy. You know that. Yes, I was weeping and I found it hard to stop. This situation. The way our lives have turned out. I have craved…intimacy. Thought it was my right. But it came to me last night. I shall never know it. Perhaps it's a myth. I hope it is a myth since I should not like to be missing out on something to which others have such easy access. It all became too much and the tears welled up. He was trying to sleep. He asked me to stop. The sniffles, the sobs, the gulping down of all this unhappiness, this disappointment, the dull ache of which deepens every day. But I could not. Stop. I ached for comfort. His scrawny pajamed arm over my chest even, his digital watch cold against my chin, to feel just his bony knee brushing against my thigh even. Small things. A knuckle on my stomach even, lips just lightly on the back of my neck even, steady life-affirming exhalations in my ear but…no, nothing. And so I wept. Sounds of the shooting and the helicopters and the screams of the wounded all around. The intrusive beams of the searchlights. But it was my stifled crying that disturbed him more. And then after a while he simply exploded.

He never wanted to resemble his father. Hates the fact that they share the same haunted look, the same asymmetrical features. Even to the way he adjusts his crotch or hawks at his nose. His father to a tee. And these traits he has worked so assiduously to eradicate. But now…they really are like peas in a pod. But you have to know the truth. Say nothing to him. He is a good man really. He has supported us well and over these long years he has made numerous astute financial investments.

I SAW MYSELF
by Howard Barker

I Saw Myself *was first performed at the Jerwood Vanbrugh Theatre, London, in April 2008.*

The play is set in thirteenth century Europe where SLEEV, the lady of the manor, has just been widowed. She and three of her ladies-in-waiting are weaving a tapestry to commemorate her husband's death in battle. However, during the course of the play, SLEEV decides to tell the truth and change the depicted story to emphasise her numerous infidelities, which renders her husband's life and death as futile. This scene takes place at the beginning of the play when all four women are working on the original version of the tapestry. SLEEV can't remember enough about her husband's face to depict it appropriately. She has a naked man concealed in her wardrobe who is also distracting her from the task in hand.

SLEEV

Four women weave a tapestry.

(*Standing abruptly.*) Again I cannot do the face
Again
Again
Again this failure with the face unpick it I can't unpick it one
of you

The women cease weaving.

Everything is against me everything against me now as ever

She turns to examine herself in the mirror of a wardrobe.
She adjusts the tilt of her hat. She opens the wardrobe door.
A naked man stands there. SLEEV *looks at him with a pained*
detachment, then she closes the door.

Why am I frustrated by the face there is a reason for this
frustration obviously the horse does not frustrate me does it
the horse also has a face

She sits again, taking up the needle.

I must confront the possibility I am not meant to do the face
at all possibly I should devote myself to the foliage
…
The landscape and the foliage
…
Yes let the servants do my husband's face and I will do the
foliage

She flings out of her chair, returns to the wardrobe and
opening the door stares at the occupant for some time before
closing the door again. She examines herself in the mirror.
She turns to the women.

The widow is of all people the least qualified to describe her
husband arguably the grief the rage and in many cases let

us admit it the sheer ecstasy combine to render her efforts grandiloquent or simply silly you know this better than me but you are too polite to say so I say polite you are in terror of my temper but we will describe your terror as politeness one of you Keshkemmity perhaps create the image of my husband his jaw his eyelids particularly and in less than five hundred stitches study my daughter if you have difficulty they shared a face do several versions then show me when I am satisfied go back and unstitch the first twelve panels

The women gasp.

Yes
Yes I yield my husband to my maid and it does not embarrass me

Smiling stiffly, SLEEV walks to her stool.

I wish to work alone now I am studying foliage foliage and drapery

The women obey, putting away their needles and going to leave. Only LADDER hesitates.

…
Alone I said

from

GET UP AND TIE YOUR FINGERS
by Ann Coburn

Get Up and Tie Your Fingers *was first performed in Eyemouth in October 1995, and throughout the Scottish Borders, by Fourth Wall Productions as part of the Borders Festival.*

On 14th October 1881 forty-five fishing boats set out from Eyemouth harbour, heart of the Scottish Borders' fishing industry. The freak storm that followed took the lives of one hundred and twenty-nine men, all from the same community. *Get Up and Tie Your Fingers* tells the story from the women's viewpoint. JANET is a widow with three sons who were all lost in the storm. Here, she describes for the audience what happened to them.

JANET

My three boys, they nearly made it home, but the gale swept their boat past the harbour mouth and onto the rocks in the bay. My boys fought so hard, but the bay was like a pot on the boil and the boat, she flipped over. Robbie and James, they clung to the hull. Robbie lost his grip first. I think – I think the heart had gone out of him when the boat hit. James, my gentle James, he reached down and grasped Robbie's arm and tried to hold him up. After the next wave, they were both gone. Angus now, my fearless boy, he made it to a rock which rises out of the bay like a finger. He hauled himself up and up until he was at the top. He hung on for an age while we struggled to reach him…but we couldnae…we couldnae… When he knew we couldnae save him and his fingers were too froze to grip the rock, he waited for the next great wave and launched himself ahead of it. My Angus leapt like a salmon, with the wave and the gale behind him. He looked so fierce and strong and he rose so high I thought he would fly right over the bay to us! I put out my arms to catch him… (*She demonstrates.*) …but then the wave curled over and crashed down and took him with it. He never rose again. (*She stops for a moment, overcome.*) When the sea delivered them up, the waves had stripped them of their clothes. All three were slimed with weed and their poor skin was purpled with bruises. Do you know what I thought when I saw them lying there? I thought of the start of their lives. Aye, that's how they came into the world – naked and purple and slippery wet. Of the twins, James was born first, and he wouldnae stop greeting until Robbie was laid against him. When they came ashore, they were together, for James had never lost his grip on Robbie's wrist. I was glad of that. My Angus now, when he was born, he leapt shouting into the world – and he left it the same way, leaping and shouting to his death! Ach, when I found him there, on the shore, it pained me to see him lie so still and quiet. Angus was never still in his life! I washed them all myself, and dressed them in their best. I held them in my arms one last time before they went to their coffins. And now, my arms… (*She holds out her arms.*) …they ache so. They willnae stop aching. They ache for something to hold, but my time for holding bairns is past. When my boys died in the bay, I saw all their bairns die with them. (*JANET remains, arms outstretched, for a few seconds. Then she bows her head.*)

From

TEJAS VERDES
by Fermín Cabal (translated by Robert Shaw)

Tejas Verdes, *written by the Spanish playwright, Fermín Cabal, was first performed in English translation at the Gate Theatre, London in January 2005.*

'Tejas Verdes' means 'Green Gables' and was the name of the detention and torture centre operated by the Chilean Army in the months following the 1973 coup by General Augusto Pinochet against the world's first democratically elected Marxist government, headed by President Salvador Allende. The coup was followed by a period of repression where some 3,000 people were 'disappeared'. The play traces the life of a young woman, Colorina, who vanished one night in Santiago. THE INFORMER was her friend but was forced to name her whilst being tortured and when her six year old son was tortured in front of her. Years later she explains what happened for the audience.

THE INFORMER

Yes, it was me who informed on her. If it hadn't been for me, she might still be alive today.

Or maybe not. It was a very long time ago.

It was her boyfriend they were after, Miguel Menéndez, a leading light in the university and my friend in the organisation. A real heavyweight.

In a way, it was me who brought them together. I'd met Colorina in Chillán, in the summer of 1970. We went there to do voluntary work to help with development in the area. I didn't care for her that much to begin with. I saw right away that she was from a rich family. Not that rich, perhaps, but she didn't go short of anything and when she went into houses and saw the misery there, she opened her eyes very wide and just stood there in silence, staring.

Then I got to like her. She was a girl who made you like her, so fine, so noble, so…delicate. I never thought they'd go as far as killing her, I thought they'd get out of her pretty fast where Miguel was and then they'd let her go, but sometimes things go wrong, the unexpected happens… Some moron was playing with a gun and it went off. The wound developed complications, they had to put her in hospital…

I'm not saying this by way of apology. What have I got to apologise for? I'm simply telling the truth: I never thought they'd go as far as killing her. Others, yes. I grassed up others knowing they'd be killed. And that they'd do dreadful things to them first. The same things they'd done to me.

If you want to judge me, please do. That's not why I'm here.

I have nothing to be ashamed of. They tortured me and I gave in. It's that simple. And till the day I die, I'll carry the wound they gave me. You see, you betray everyone around you, your own people. Anyone you've loved, men you've been in love with, your friends, your family if you have to. And they know who to ask you about, because when you do give in, the more pain they cause you, the more you submit.

I open up my photo album and start turning the pages and there they all are, staring at me.

From

WHAT THE NIGHT IS FOR
by Michael Weller

What the Night is For *was first produced by Act Productions, Sonia Friedman Productions and LHP at the Comedy Theatre, London, in November 2002.*

Ten years after the end of their affair in New York, Adam and LINDY meet in a bland Midwestern hotel room for dinner. Both are in their mid to late forties and married with children but their passion for each other hasn't died. The night reveals their hopes, dreams and regrets. In this speech, LINDY explains how she felt after she left New York, and Adam.

LINDY

Adam, you don't know…you can't begin to imagine how on the edge / I was *lost* after New York. Do you understand? Not immediately, not *right* after, but… (*Thinks back.*) Actually it was just a *sadness* at first, very slight. Which I took to be…the lack of a lover. I'd never had one before you, so I didn't know the signs. And I figured, okay, maybe what I need is someone to replace you, and practical-minded Lindy that I am, I found, *chose* actually, with cold-blooded calculation – poor man – the Curator of the Plains Indian Museum. I'm on the board, so no eyebrows rose over the odd meeting. And he was discrete, attentive…a thoroughly adequate choice, except for his aftershave, which smelled like banana. Not an erotic scent, I discovered. The problem was, nothing about him felt *necessary*. And this vague sadness inside, it was still there. So I ended it one day. Very cordial, 'Au revoir, thanks for the sex, see you at the next board meeting.' Then out in the parking lot I started towards my car and…collapsed. Fell down in the snow desolate. Thinking of you. Buried under this tidal wave of grief.

And with a family to manage. I had to schedule suffering between dishes and laundry. God save anyone from going through what I had to getting over you – without letting it show. Waking the kids. Making breakfast, packing lunch, getting them off to school in time to drive somewhere alone and lie down behind the steering wheel sobbing. Making love to your husband when every inch of you feels numb. Watching him move over you, and collapse, and you feel nothing at all.

She faces him now.

I'll never put myself through that again.

From

ON LOVE
by Mick Gordon

On Love *was first performed as Love's Work at the Gate Theatre, London in November 2000.*

On Love is a collection of love stories. Hundreds of people were interviewed on their individual experiences of love and the most resonant and touching were workshopped into a play or 'theatre essay'. Here, GABRIELLE talks about the birth of her son.

GABRIELLE

I can remember the birth of my first child, my son, I remember it absolutely. My mother always said to me, you won't remember giving birth, that's the great thing about it, you don't remember it. Well I think she was so full of drugs and gas that she couldn't remember. Well when I did it, you didn't do that, I wanted a natural birth, so I stuck it out without any drugs at all, not even a Paracetamol and I can remember it in excruciating detail. And the moment that I first saw my son. Absolutely clearly. But the thing is, is, when they're inside you, you don't have any image of an um…child, it's just a lump, it's not a person. And then amazingly, when it comes out. Well I was lying there and they handed it to me and there was this little person. It took me completely by surprise. Actually last night I was thinking, erm, Neal, my son, is seventeen now, he's doing his A-levels and he's applying to go to university. And last night I was thinking, in a year's time he'll be gone. This time next year he won't be at home any more. He's doing a gap year in Vietnam. Teaching English. In Vietnam! But that little person who was handed to me, I can still see the embryo in my great big gangling boy. I can still see that little baby in him. But in a year's time he'll be gone.

From

THE ERROR OF THEIR WAYS
by Torben Betts

The Error of their Ways *was first performed in August 2007 at the HERE Arts Center, New York.*

ELIZABETH is described as a beautiful but cold widow whose husband, a politician, was brutally assassinated in his professional prime. He briefly revived in the morgue but she quickly (and secretly) strangled him to ensure her future success and independence. After meeting her husband's assassin, for whom she feels overwhelming desire, she takes her husband's place as leader. This is her speech to the people from a balcony on the occasion of her husband's funeral.

ELIZABETH

A balcony. A coffin. The screaming of a celebratory crowd.
ELIZABETH *steps forward, dressed in black. The screaming*
and cheering increases. With one hand she quietens the
people.

For your applause and your love…for your unbridled rejoicing
this day…I thank you. This overflowing of joy is as a balm to
my grieving soul. From the depths of my being I thank you
for it. (*Aside.*) Such an ocean of grey. And such a myriad of
sweating pates. One observes the patches of baldness, these
ludicrous specks of pink as they flash out from under the
swelling banners. (*To the crowd.*) I pledge to you this day, this
day which is a triumph of democracy, I pledge to you this day,
my people, that this country of ours, which for so long has
been neglected by those elected to govern it, that this country
will again come to represent all that is good, all that is true
and all that is decent in the world today.

Huge cheering.

(*Aside.*) I cannot deny there is an energy flowing. Their insane
bellowing is having a startling effect upon me. I am becoming
intoxicated with the thrill of celebrity. Oh, yes. I can say
anything, anything. (*To the crowd.*) I speak to you now as a
woman who is at the most tender, the most vulnerable stage
in her life.

The crowd falls into a respectful silence.

I have reached an age where a woman has brought up her
children and seen them launch themselves into what we all
know can be a brutal and terrifying world. Their going has
pained me. (*Aside.*) How pleased was I to have their loutish
swaggering, their back-patting stupidity finally out of my
house. (*To the crowd.*) However, I have also reached an age

where a woman can look back on her achievements, be they at home or in the workplace, and she can, if she has lived wisely, look back with pride and with a serene smile on her face. My husband and I were looking forward to a new chapter, yes, a new phase of existence where we were together going to ensure that the privileges and happinesses we have enjoyed would one day become the birthright of all.

A murmur of sympathy from the crowd.

But you know of course that this is now not to be. I have been robbed of my soulmate, my love, my dear friend, when we were together about to effect a magnificent change in this extraordinary land of ours. And so my heart is naturally heavy with grief, my eyes filled with bitter tears, my soul in a profound sadness every moment of every day… And yet…this pain is now a little assuaged by a feeling of extreme optimism, Yes, though I come here today to bury my husband, I am also here to resurrect the nation. It is my dearest hope that my husband's passing may serve as a symbol to all of us. May we all, though his body lies cold and lifeless in this coffin, may we all struggle to rebuild our communities and to love one another as good Christian men and women should, so as to keep alive the memory of my husband's ideas, his vision of compassion and social reform.

A wave of enthusiasm through the crowd.

Your love, as I say, is something I cherish during this, the hour of my deepest desolation.

Forgive me for a moment…for I am quite overwhelmed.

From

ROOM TO LET
by Paul Tucker

Room to Let *was first performed at the Chelsea Centre Theatre, London, in May 1999.*

JANET is 48 years old and has lived with her partner, Eddie, for 24 years. Eddie isn't JANET's ideal man and she spends a great deal of time abusing him. Despite this, she still wants to marry him as she's always wanted to be married. She has decided to rent out the spare room so that there will be enough money for the wedding and a honeymoon at Butlins in Bognor. Unfortunately Eddie isn't keen and, later on in the play, we learn that Eddie has already been married but walked out on his wife and child many years ago. Here, JANET introduces herself to the audience.

JANET

I'm Janet, I'm 48, live with me partner, Eddie, been living together now for 24 years. Twenty-four years too long if you ask me. Met through Lonely Hearts, and I must have been lonely to meet him. Idle bleeder, he don't wanna go work, don't wanna take me on holiday, don't wanna do nought for me. He drives me mad sometimes, he aint got any get up and go, lazy. I've been waiting all these years for him to take me up the aisle. I mean, it's a girl's dream to get a ring on her finger, isn't it? That's why we're getting a lodger in, so we can have some money to pay for the honeymoon and such – cause he won't go out and earn it. I have to go out and earn, just a cleaning job at the infirmary, mind. We put an ad in the Post Office window last week, but no bugger's come to look at the room. Even if they did, they'd take one look at him, and leave. It isn't that I don't love Eddie, I mean, you get used to someone after all these years, you live and breathe 'em. I'd say I love him but I'm not in love with him if you get me meaning. I have to boss him around sometimes to motivate him, he's got no get up and go in him. I feel more like his mother at times than his wife. I aint lying but if I went away for a week, I'd come back and the house would look like a pigsty. I should have known from the start on our first date. He never had any money then and he hasn't got any money now. I had to buy the rounds! I know these days, a couple share rounds and stuff but in those days, it wasn't done for the woman to buy everything! His suit was all scruffy, he had bits of car oil over his shirt. He's the same now as he was then…

From

THE BIGGLESWADES
by Torben Betts

The Biggleswades *was first produced at the White Bear Theatre, London in November 2001.*

Brian Biggleswade is obsessive and paranoid, barricading himself and his submissive WIFE against the terror of the outside world, creating a world of rituals and routines that, ultimately, stifles her. He has been waiting, all his life, for something extraordinary, something fantastic to happen to him and this anticipation keeps him moving forward. However, his WIFE has wearied of the rituals and the waiting. This speech is one of the few moments in her life when she speaks out against him.

THE WIFE

Do you remember the days when we first met? Do you? Can you cast your mind back to those halcyon days, those carefree days when our futures stretched out before us like a clear blue river on a lovely summer's day? (*No answer.*) Because I can. I was just thinking of them. Those days. And you…I can see you now. Your face, your little child-like face with all its pretty innocence. Little hopeful beady eyes. Sweet little giggle. You had such a glow about you. A little golden glow, grinning with health and happiness. And it was then, when we sat down after a dance…we danced a lot in those days, Brian…it was then that you told me of the event that was to befall you, the overwhelming revelation that was to alter your life forever. Something momentous, something fantastic. It was going to light up your days and tie up all the loose ends. Wasn't it, Brian? Hmm? (*A pause.*) And you took me into your confidence. You said you needed a friend, a loyal friend to accompany you, to hold your hand through the endless hours of your search. (*A pause.*) And all those days. All those long, long days. Day after day after day after day. Each one running into the next. All those days. Those days, those days and still they pass. In a constant stream. A constant stream of day changing into night, of night changing into day, of day into night, of night into day, of day into night, of night into day, of day….

From

THE LADY OF BURMA
by Richard Shannon

The Lady of Burma *first previewed as part of a Gala presentation at the Old Vic Theatre, London in November 2006. The first performance took place at the Edinburgh Festival Fringe in August 2007.*

This one-woman play tells the extraordinary story of Burmese pro-democracy leader and Nobel Peace Prize Laureate AUNG SAN SUU KYI in her own words. It opens with AUNG SAN SUU KYI imprisoned by the Burmese military junta in Rangoon jail. She plunges back into the past, piecing events together, speaking directly to the audience. She remembers returning to Burma so that she can nurse her dying mother, leaving her husband and children in England. A young man visits her to see if she will support the students against the government; however, their 'peaceful' rally goes horribly wrong.

AUNG SAN SUU KYI

I hear the gunfire from the verandah. Machine gun fire –
– relentless –
And the distant cries of the dying.

It seems to go on for at least an hour – then it stops – only to
be heard again, intermittently – like brush fires catching – as
the Tatmadaw hunt down any students who had escaped their
first deadly volleys.
I sit on the steps of my mother's house – frozen.

SUU sinks to knees and sits.

Then the persistent young man is at my side – covered in
blood – sweat coursing down his face, blackened with dust.
He is shaking.
He grips my arm and tells me again and again:

(*As the young man.*) 'They're killing everyone…they're all
dead…it's not safe…it's not…it's…'

Then he sinks to his knees and weeps.
I hold him. I hold him as he rocks backwards and forwards.
Until there are no tears left.
I order tea and a bowl of water.

SUU bathes the imaginary young man.

I ask him to tell me exactly what has happened.

He speaks very slowly at first and keeps his eyes firmly fixed
on the ground.

He tells me he is responsible – he had organised the students.

He had printed the leaflets…printed them from wax blocks
and rolled them out with fluorescent tubes. His group
– the fighting red peacock – was responsible…but the

demonstration was peaceful…they just sat down…sat down in the square, in front of the Town Hall.
Just sat down.

His eyes blink away tears.

SUU enters the memory.

They are sitting in the baking sun.

Hours pass.

They begin to chant…

We hear the students chanting.

(*As the students.*) 'Partizo democrazi senet tu do ye – Do ye! Do ye!
Democracy – it is people's business – Do ye! Do ye!
Panzi jaona pianloye, Do ye! Do ye!
Release all political prisoners – Do ye! Do ye!

They even share their food with the soldiers guarding the Town Hall, as the hours wear on.
Then someone shouts – 'They're coming!'

We hear tanks and soldiers in the distance.

In the distance, they hear the thrum of engines and the clank of caterpillar tracks – plumes of dirty diesel smoke puncture the air as the tanks and armoured cars close off all the exits to the square.

From

MARLENE
by Pam Gems

Marlene *was first performed at the Oldham Coliseum Theatre in October 1996 and opened at the Lyric Theatre, Shaftesbury Avenue, London, in April 1997.*

The legendary actress, MARLENE DIETRICH, has just arrived in Paris and is preparing for her evening's solo performance. She is now in her seventies and at the end of her career. This monologue is set in her backstage dressing room, where she reflects on the horrors of touring. 'V' is Vivian Hoffman who is acting as her personal assistant.

MARLENE

They have no idea. 'Oh, Miss Dietrich! Welcome to Rio, London, Sydney! SO good to see you again!' (*Sotto voce.*) 'Look at her – fifth world tour!… schlepping around the world and back again – what for?' 'Oh, you know, these old movie stars, it's like a drug to them…they need the applause.'

Like hell.

I need the money. (*Shrugs.*) AND the applause.

Now Paris. The only city for a woman. Yah, but for Paris you must be wonderful. Wonderful? After ten hours on a plane eating purple food, ankles swollen and not seeing so good? I need oxygen! Now the hotel says the penthouse is not available. The President of the World Bank is here. With his entourage. Entourage! Yah… I met her last year in Gstaad.

(*Calls.*) V! Call to the Shah of Persia – the number is in the blue book – tell him I need a small favour.

We'll leak a little Persian oil, give the World Bank a fright.

Hotels! Horror stories, more like. Airlines all the same logo – 'Luggage to follow'. Can you believe where was my big trunk last week? Kuala Lumpur. 'Oh, Miss Dietrich, your lovely dresses! Lovely dresses!' (*Shakes her head.*) Uch-uch. You know what's inside? Electrical adaptors. When you are touring as long as me you don't take a chance. Yah…agents, managers…fog, strike, crisis – 'Take the Concorde, be here yesterday'…in the end, your work, the thing you dedicated your life to, denied yourself, lost friends for…the work – that becomes remote…immaterial. Only real thing is this mindless, endless, toxic voyage in space. You know what I am in the end – a long-distance truck driver.

So different from the old days. Hollywood…nineteen thirty. City of dreams for the whole world. And you know – it was just a sleepy little village, on the edge of nowhere. But so beautiful…to look out at the Pacific, always shining, orange groves right down to the sea – Oh and the air! Like Beaume de Venise! Ultimate accolade. To be summoned to Hollywood. I never forget that first sea voyage. How to travel! Fine staterooms, orchestras, champagne, wonderful food out of this world, and every passenger on board talented, beautiful… everyone exciting.

I remember one day on deck this American woman – so lovely, the face, the neck – dark hair, blue eyes, like the Irish. The third night, after the cabaret, we are standing by the rail, and so I kiss the neck. Why not? My God! The scandal!

She was lovely. A bit like Greta Garbo only – you know – good looking.

Grrreta Garrrbo. Always on the screen like she is suffering some female problem down below. How can you be so blue all the time? Well, yoghurt and mung beans, what do you expect?

The phone rings.

(*Bawls.*) V! Get it, I don't take calls in the dressing room.

The Books

THE LAST VALENTINE
by Glyn Maxwell
from *Plays Two*

ISBN 978-1-84002-615-3

**HANNAH AND HANNA
VIRGINS
RISK**
by John Retallack
from *Company of Angels*

ISBN 978-1-84002-725-9

BLACK CROWS
by Linda Brogan

ISBN 978-1-84002-737-2

ROSALIND
by Deborah Gearing

ISBN 978-1-84002-659-7

**THE MURDERS AT ARGOS
CRESSIDA AMONG THE
GREEKS**
by David Foley

ISBN 978-1-84002-323-7

BREATHING CORPSES
by Laura Wade

ISBN 978-1-84002-546-0

SMALL MIRACLE
by Neil D'Souza

ISBN 978-1-84002-784-6

**STAMPING, SHOUTING AND
SINGING HOME**
by Lisa Evans

ISBN 978-1-84002-703-7

**A BRIEF HISTORY OF
HELEN OF TROY**
by Mark Schultz

ISBN 978-1-84002-634-4

NAVY PIER
by John Corwin

ISBN 978-1-84002-199-8

GLASS EELS
by Nell Leyshon

ISBN 978-1-84002-753-2

LOVE AND MONEY
by Dennis Kelly
from *Plays One*

ISBN 978-1-84002-695-5

LA CASA AZUL
by Sophie Faucher,
translated by Neil
Bartlett

ISBN 978-1-84002-348-0

TALKING TO TERRORISTS
by Robin Soans

ISBN 978-1-84002-562-0

CAMILLE
adapted by Neil
Bartlett from *La
Dame aux camélias* by
Alexandre Dumas *fils*

ISBN 978-1-84002-360-2

JAMAICA INN
adapted by Lisa Evans
from the novel by
Daphne du Maurier

ISBN 978-1-84002-409-8

GUARDIANS
by Peter Morris

ISBN 978-1-84002-642-9

THE BOGUS WOMAN
by Kay Adshead

ISBN 978-1-84002-209-4

THE EUROPEANS
by Howard Barker

from *Plays One*

ISBN 978-1-84002-612-2

SLEEPING DOGS
by Philip Osment

from *Plays for Young
People*

ISBN 978-1-84002-272-8

INCARCERATOR
by Torben Betts

from *Plays Two*

ISBN 978-1-84002-200-1

ONCE WE WERE MOTHERS
by Lisa Evans

ISBN 978-1-84002-499-9

THE WAR NEXT DOOR
by Tamsin Oglesby

ISBN 978-1-84002-729-7

**THE DARKER FACE OF THE
EARTH**
by Rita Dove

ISBN 978-1-84002-129-5

TAKING CARE OF BABY
by Dennis Kelly

ISBN 978-1-84002-778-5

LATER
by David Pownell

from *Plays for One Person*

ISBN 978-1-84002-010-6

VICTORY AT THE DIRT PALACE
by Adriano Shaplin

from *Three Plays*

ISBN 978-1-84002-489-0

SUFFERING THE WITCH
by David Foley

ISBN 978-1-84002-473-9

13 OBJECTS: SOUTH OF THAT PLACE NEAR
by Howard Barker

from *Plays Four*

ISBN 978-1-84002-648-1

LIFE AFTER LIFE
by Paul Jepson and Tony Parker

ISBN 978-1-84002-301-5

PICASSO'S WOMEN
by Brian McAvera

ISBN 978-1-870259-86-6

FALLING
by Shelley Silas

ISBN 978-1-84002-328-2

FEVER
by Reza de Wet

ISBN 978-1-84002-492-0

A WOMAN IN WAITING
by Yael Farber and Thembi Mtshali-Jones

from *Theatre as Witness*

ISBN 978-1-84002-820-1

I LIKE MINE WITH A KISS
by Georgia Fitch

ISBN 978-1-84002-724-2

A NEW YORK THREESOME: MANHATTAN BREAST COMPANY
by Lesley Ross

from *The Jolly Folly of Polly, the Scottish Trolley Dolly and other mini-marvels*

ISBN 978-1-84002-541-5

THE UNCONQUERED
by Torben Betts

ISBN 978-1-84002-723-5

I SAW MYSELF
by Howard Barker

from *Plays Four*

ISBN 978-1-84002-851-5

THE ERROR OF THEIR WAYS
by Torben Betts

ISBN 978-1-84002-801-0

GET UP AND TIE YOUR FINGERS
by Ann Coburn

ISBN 978-1-84002-114-1

ROOM TO LET
by Paul Tucker

ISBN 978-1-84002-125-7

TEJAS VERDES
by Fermin Cabal, translated by Robert Shaw

ISBN 978-1-84002-537-8

THE BIGGLESWADES
by Torben Betts

from *Plays Two*

ISBN 978-1-84002-200-1

WHAT THE NIGHT IS FOR
by Michael Weller

ISBN 978-1-84002-355-8

THE LADY OF BURMA
by Richard Shannon

ISBN 978-1-84002-786-0

ON LOVE
by Mick Gordon

ISBN 978-1-84002-608-5

MARLENE
by Pam Gems

ISBN 978-1-84002-064-9